Other books by Lyn Hejinian:

A Thought Is the Bride of What Thinking (Tuumba, 1976)
A Mask of Motion (Burning Deck, 1977)
Gesualdo (Tuumba, 1978)
Writing Is an Aid to Memory (The Figures, 1978)
My Life (Burning Deck, 1980)
The Guard (Tuumba, 1984)
Redo (Salt Works Press, 1984)
My Life (revised edition; Sun & Moon, 1987)
Individuals (with Kit Robinson; Chax Press, 1988)
Leningrad (with Michael Davidson, Ron Silliman, and Barrett Watten;
    Mercury House, 1991)
The Hunt (Zasterle Press, 1991)
The Cell (Sun & Moon, 1991)

OXOTA: A SHORT RUSSIAN NOVEL

LYN HEJINIAN

for Lauren,

"Hoops of desire are spun around reason"

love, Andrew

The Figures

Individual poems from this book have been published in *Five Fingers Review*, *fragmente*, *Grand Street*, *Hot Bird Mfg*, *Meanjin*, *o-blēk*, *Pequod*, *The Poetry Project Newsletter*, *Raddle Moon*, and *Writing*, and the author is very grateful to the editors of these magazines for their interest and encouragement.

"Book Five" was published by Manuel Brito's Zasterle Press (Tenerife, Canary Islands) under the title *The Hunt*. A selection of poems from throughout this book has been translated into French and will be published by Cahiers de Royaumont under the title *Le Jour de Chasse*.

The Banff Centre for the Arts provided the time and place in which this book was finished, and the author gratefully acknowledges this support.

Finally and especially, thanks to Elena Balashova; to Gannon Hall; to Arkadii Dragomoshchenko for contributing to this book and all that surrounds it, and for chapter 109 which consists almost entirely of sentences translated and mistranslated from his letters to the author; to Zina Dragomoshchenko; to Ostap Dragomoshchenko for the cover painting and for many real and imaginary paintings within it; to Steve Lacy for chapters 71-80 and chapters 261-270; to Barrett Watten; and both here and beyond the book to Larry Ochs.

The Figures, 5 Castle Hill, Great Barrington, MA 01230
Distributed by *Small Press Distribution*, *Sun & Moon*, *Segue*, *Inland Book Company*, *Bookslinger*, and by Paul Green in the UK. Publication of this book is supported by a grant from the National Endowment for the Arts, Literature Program, and by a gift from the *Fund for Poetry*.
Cover type by Brita Bergland
Printed by Thomson-Shore, Inc., of Dexter, MI
ISBN 0-935724-44-3
ISBN 0-935724-48-6 (signed)

for Zina

Book One

Chapter One

This time we are both
The old thaw is inert, everything set again in snow
At insomnia, at apathy
We must learn to endure the insecurity as we read
The felt need for a love intrigue
There is no person — he or she was appeased and withdrawn
There is relationship but it lacks simplicity
People are very aggressive and every week more so
The Soviet colonel appearing in such of our stories
He is sentimental and duckfooted
He is held fast, he is in his principles
But here is a small piece of the truth — I am glad to greet you
There, just with a few simple words it is possible to say the
    truth
It is so because often men and women have their sense of
    honor

Chapter Two

No form at all—it's impossible to imagine its being seen from
   above
Nor sense of time because work is only done discontinuously
I had no sense of making an impression
The blue shadows of footprints and a diffuse pink or green
   light between them on the saturated park were soaking
   the snow
A reflection of the violent word MIR painted green was
   mirrored warped on a stretch of deserted ice
All my memories then as Leningrad lay like the shallow sheets
   of water banked by rubble and melting snow which
   covered the field in a northern housing district of the city
   across which we were often walking toward the housing
   blocks in winter, its surface wildly broken by the light
Something impossible to freeze, or the very lack of thing
Dusk as it continued to be
In the evenings particularly we made notes and took dictation
   in anticipation of writing a short Russian novel, something
   neither invented nor constructed but moving through
   that time as I experienced it unable to take part
   personally in the hunting
Taking patience and suddenness—even sleeping in
   preparedness, in sadness
No paper for books
I had lost all sense of forming expressions
No paper at all in the south, and the butcher stuffs pieces of
   greasy black beef into the women's purses
Other links exist, on other levels, between our affairs

Chapter Three

Something hangs in the drawing room and it's green
A painted herring hung where it's harder to recognize
I slept there in a corner on the sofa called America
In a bed near the Vyborg by a crowbar with a magpie-dog duo
    singing a ballad without the neighbor's shaking out his
    blanket
I dreamed I was walking somewhere in the Crimea with my
    mother when we met two soldiers and their man in
    handcuffs
He was a criminal of passion
The riddle depending on delayed recognition of a thing like a
    herring—Armenian
A maiden name
A visa
I answered the top man at the consulate and said the word was
    marital
Rubble—so you see that our people must squat in their ditch
    and speak of beauty
The enemy freezes to its trees
The old women who survived had to have been witches, said
    Misha
Bitches, said Arkadii Trofimovich—the crime of passion is our
    Soviet kindness

Chapter Four

A person's hypersensitivity is no longer witty
And in the Russian novel is an obverse of a person
A complete entity with a voice its own droning with its nose
pressed against the wall
The wall was intuitively placed between the breasts
Not having possession but being pressed
And we are conscientious
With age one ought to gain something besides weight
Height
Adherence
There's a lot of waiting in the drama of experience
Now cold is suddenly springing from the floorboards
Travellers buying the brooms of birches
More than once as I write you'll find yourself reading of the
weather and Leningrad light
The next morning it was minus 8 degrees and our sense of the
    passage of time was mild since our time had no
    destination

Chapter Five

We are occupied with production, but these are our times of
     mute people
A dim housing block the substance of igloo
A sleep somewhere between crumbling and construction
A thing called sleep
A dream in which Stalin enters it
People are told to renovate the means by which they satisfy
     their material wants and that's not art
All light ruins white
Whom then to love
What
How could one love one's life if it were new
The famous emigre is a bourgeois lyricist
Why not, said Lydia Yakovlevna
To the post office, then the apothecary
If there can be socialist realism then there can surely be
     bourgeois lyricism

Chapter Six

Arkadii Trofimovitch wrote from 1:30 to 3
White and no degree
Enormous angry crows and furious magpies waited for a dog
    under the trees
With a name like Polkan to be called
A colonel on the snow past babushkas on their bench with the
    mineral water culled from iron
He will pull off his huge coat to cover the child on the rails
A sentence and its passivity
Its metonymy
Then Vitya arrived — slow discussion with him
Effacement, orientation, the syllogism, retardation
I can't say whether the person was appeased or never existed
About something which is nothing, for example, we can say
We can say he is . . . he is don't-sew-a-sleeve-to-a-cunt
Fixed white

Chapter Seven

One person believes in nothing and another dislikes poetry
They don't present equal dangers to society
The lowness of the light stole the field from its shadows
An old babushka on the ice atop the ridge of snow packed
  beside the street
In deed and word
She was hissing
And a pedestrian screaming, what are doing up there, you
  stupid old woman
The shouting samaritan jerked the granny to safety
She was hissing like a street cat, not snakily
An engine, an omen of weddings
An habitual association with daily aesthetic impressions
An omen of the love of art and its social functioning
An orb standing for an orbit
The old woman still standing in the street

Chapter Eight

This is not seen as something else
This is not scene—not in a dramatic sense
Standing as a voluptuary, developed in a wooden box
Clutched from frost
Well, I would like to lose all my bad habits, but never in my life
    have I had so little opportunity for doing so
Gray or white with objectivity which slides out written
At times human experiences appear more dramatic to others
    than they do to the person who is having them but as if
    waiting
As if lacking a self to improve
An instrumental
I am settled in the shadows at the corner of the bed
I am reprimanded by Zina that the light is bad
But I had nothing to link to it
A sex static and tingling of oblivion and description
The child of my father but not me

Chapter Nine

There is room in Pushkin's small house at Pavlovsk and it's the
    same yellow
Somewhat sentimental or really so after the palace
Sentimental asides
The locking of asides
Snow was falling in the yard around a hard currency hospital
    of the same color
The rubles too as thick as snowflakes
And here at my window, said Arkadii Trofimovich, is my West
But where was Pushkin's bed
He can't decide what he decides
Two anti-Semites thundering about "north guys" and "blue
    eyes" and "black guys"
They were drumming on Sasha's side
His face was pale, the skin thin and dry, his eyes full but of
    what he couldn't say, asleep and awake, awful nights
More idiots! said the colonel, almost catching the intonation
    of the cab driver
Pushkin remains himself, but what self has he to remain

Chapter Ten

Misha, we too will submit to our lot
There's a false opposition between art and reality
Misha!
Ho! answered Misha
Your brain wouldn't even serve as a file folder
A false correspondence with life
You're right, Mitya—it contains too little and yet it contains
    too much
But it's naive to refuse to acknowledge that one thing is art
    and another belongs to reality (and let's assume that
    there's only reality)
The sense of accumulation, and of the increase of
    probability—there are no opposites
There's no sense in worrying about imitation, since a situation
    after enough time can't help but sit and increase as it does
Agoraphobic and sweating, people swollen in buses
A schoolboy submitted among thighs to the swelling and slept
Under cat steam, within cabbage
I hate to leave a place just before, during, or immediately after
    a storm

Chapter Eleven

With exhilarating humility we watched the accumulating snow
The shifting of greenish drifts, the yellow silent wind
Not defiant but obsequious in storm, at kitchen window
Money is not unlucky
But a whistling man is luckless in money
What then if snow is the substance of an accounting
No objects of metonymy, of economy
A colonel's daughter drew in the frost like a vandal to the
    colonel
The wolves whistled in the forest near Pavlovsk
Little Dima bravely raced toward the palace parking lot
A poetry and with fear of authority — as if that were your sole
    justification, in itself, not in what you wrote
Simple being — simple agoraphobic being
Its meals
Their daily huntress

Chapter Twelve

Almost blue horseradish in great sadness
Mute painting and articulate painter
The colonel said to his wife that they were cutting his pay to
        cover the cost of a panzer tank he'd lost in a maneuver
Well, Misha said, as they say, you slide down the slope bare-
        assed and stop yourself with your prick
Siberia starts twenty minutes from there
Slivers of meat whittled from a frozen slab stored on the
        windowsill
But with an incomplete gesture, an unfinished phrase
We are among things on which reality has been slowly settling
        and is then dusted away
An hour after power soup, pieces of an unfamiliar fish and
        pickles scattered over rice
The second smoke in Soviet cooking is a blue one
Smoke, condiment, and bread
They are enclosed in such simple understanding that going
        out right then for milk involved an unintelligible belief in
        everything
I simply couldn't manage the incorporation of what I know —
        or was in the process of knowing
As they say, black is a color that glitters, and blue is a black that
        doesn't glitter

Chapter Thirteen

The sleeves of the dress and the spread
Your back is beautiful, he had said
Ahead of memory
Sulfur sifting through the lines
Pale rocks, the size of eggs
I remembered riding a sledge between horses' legs
Gavronsky, inflated with pleasure, had his back turned
Arkadii Trofimovich waded through the mud
The old woman never tethered the goat, he said, her husband
    at the window yelling for his pay
The old woman took her wine with her mouth to the mud
If there are nationalists there is a city, an enthusiastic sum
Ahead of meat
And women with or without sympathy, are they in lines
Spoons

Chapter Fourteen

Women do have sense of humor
And sense of utensil — steaming bus
Things bringing our being into proximity with themselves
A woman interesting a man in herself because of what women
    like
There are letters and place
One could long for someone right there with one and not be
    able to eat at all
That is a transition, or a desire for one
It's most contemporary when in the least time it covers the
    greatest space
Nothing muffled in memory
It was a day without anything's seeming to have priority
And many of the people were simply stolid, suspicious not by
    habit but by design
While waiting to see how much could change, it couldn't
    repeat itself but we could
Nothing in sequence, nothing in consequence
The same thing happens every day and then one day it fails to
    happen

Chapter Fifteen

As emotional as the thumb, and beyond it the sun
Rose snow fell
The sun was only at thumb height
The river, the never
Over Nevsky a city that doesn't sit — in light that never gathers
Enormous, gorgeous — your thumb
It isn't patience because it isn't waiting
Society and upon it tattoo
The thumb is not nature
No more have I thought
Nor youth
But diameter I have, and the thumb for adherence
It is not a career, not in our sense
In our difference

Chapter Sixteen

The chance unsettled, though I was really trying to do so
Snow, minus two degrees
A paper falls to the floor and its author must sit on it
We must all sit again before going a distance
But I think it's not orthodox
I was thinking of an awful eroticism, even of prison
Then the colonel, a man from the village, for the first time
    travels from the provinces
He arrives safely in Leningrad by train and takes a cab
He sweats down his cheeks from his fur hat
Without conclusion
Three Vanyas living on a farm — long Vanya, flat Vanya, and
    doctor Ivan
Another idiot, mutters the cab driver, another idiot
A draft of an opinion of poverty
It is winter and the kidneys are blooming

Chapter Seventeen

Let's consider subjectivity but relieved of self
It's like a child — all eyes
Or gun — the new mafia has guns
His mafia, said Sergei — but mine would know him
It's not expensive at all: 500 rubles, 1000 for someone
    important
A magnificent stairway to a small overhang — in the corners
    the Masons met
Pierre — I don't know one of this name
Pashka in Africa
Afrika
Jews and Masons — they are the responsible ones
North guys are good guys with blue eyes
The sashlik repulsive — I covered my eyes — Zina said, "Little
    guys . . ."
I drank 2 tablespoons of uva ursi tea and ate a digestive pill
"Little sons," she said, "it isn't our Soviet problem to get these
    Western guys killed"

Chapter Eighteen

My yellow is translucent in its Cuban grapefruit
The knife of solicitude, the invasion of solace
One is hesitant by intruding
A man says, say something, it's a sex of inquiry
It's the subvocalization of bed, or of nest
Of America
Slava was insisting that I should bomb Cuba
You should
It's Soviet
Did they fascinate that
Do we separate it
There was a big field on which a Ghanese guy was kicking, and
      a great crowd thickening, thinking
I remember it as heartening (Castro was there)
I remember it as beatnik

Chapter Nineteen

No stop
Proponents of necessity in defiance of mud
What of the history we take
What are you saying! says the damp colonel
Can you answer riddles?
Of course I can
The son of my father but not me, who is it
Minus 3 degrees, white frost on the trees — realism is very
    optimistic
What is warranted
The old director at the Film Institute rises from his chair and
    drops to the floor to sit on a filmstrip
The rejection of transparency
Three hundred drummers inducing pregnancy
Our result was Ivan the Terrible, Dima said
O.k., I don't know

Chapter Twenty

At night the nightingale will torment us with its mercurial
    phosphorescent singing
Yet again propagandists are saying they must drain St.
    Petersburg
They want to build a dike and block a conduit
Still, said Arkadii, I've never been drawn to the soil
So my mother says I'm a true bastard
A dream
Brine, ozone
Our swamp sleeps in our cellars
Sleep is the cutting edge of inertia
I received compensation for the insomnia which had bothered
    me for weeks, but awake I wasn't alert — in fact, I was
    nervous and suppressed
Yet both awake and asleep the process of translating matter
    into memory continued
Americans have an inexorable urge to be confessional — but
    they seldom speak confidentially, preferring to be
    overheard
Even during their American dream
With tongues for streets

Chapter Twenty-One

Dreams don't understand, they're what's being understood
A commentator in the kitchen on television gives the official
    explanation that the reason there's no food in the stores
    is that people are eating too much
But the television is only a three-inch square
Rice with horseradish and bread
We had bought some daffodils and had taped the petals erect
Following Zina I had felt slightly exposed, but as a child does
    out of bed
She had previously enraged a group of the enormous
    courtyard crows
A face they heard
No installments
We proposed a film called "Neighbor"
The man from the joint-venture "Vidium" said he could pay a
    Soviet crew in chewing gum
Then we went to a party at Misha's — potatoes with mushrooms,
    two different cabbage salads, wine, vodka, and bread
The conversation in stages of anecdote
A granny with kolbasa, Zina, the poor dog with pecked eyes,
    and the crows

Chapter Twenty-Two

We were shuffling with a man of one blue
The symmetry of the Pribaltiskaya loomed
And the Gulf of Finland under Lenin's hand hung —
    shimmering, humid, gray-green, beyond brooms
Gavronsky stood with his back to the gulf
On the street stood a deracinated nationalist with a butterfly
    bomb
The kid knowing that he knows, but not yet known as he is
    known
My brother! the cab driver told the colonel
I am suddenly oppressed
It is sky and the blue is yelping
Elegy
I couldn't dispute
There is no soap
There is no failure
It is not imperfect

Chapter Twenty-Three

An elegy is continuous
It is slow and not alarmed
Like a colonel's vacation, it reroutes objects toward their
        common unexpected end
The end is temporary
But the people are so exhausted
But this is a novel, in the literature of context
The culture of our placing places
Language put it here and us within it
When the colonel went back to the provinces, everyone came
        to his flat
More idiots! he said
And ordinary philologists might repeat that across the kitchen
        table
Zina said, put your microscope here, Vitya, and let's look at a
        drop of water, or anything, I don't know what
This is like looking a dead man in the eye, said Dima
That's an ism, said Mitya

Chapter Twenty-Four

Above the humid gulf of Finland, blinded on a balcony
In the kitchen Tanya was cooking to "sounds of Soviet reggae"
Sergei asked about nigger music
You mean, I said — Black
And I see you're pink, he raged then — yes, is that your
    color? — and maybe yellow too — it disgusts me — it's
    like chicken fat
He was pleased with that
Sergei says you're a racist, Mitya told me later — he heard you
    calling niggers black
Niggers?
As Faulkner says — it's a literary word, respectful, yes?
Meanwhile Sveta lay on the sofa
St. Petersburg, she said in English
Tanya was eating butter
On the gulf lay a mist of azure, buzzing
The glare was casting — or the overcast was glare

Chapter Twenty-Five

I could never regret a cognition, but it was of an incident
We were backstage at customs
Dove blue, badly stitched, in an airport with nothing indicative
Minerals and cosmetics — everything begrudged
All things are new pants
An elk ran by
By not naming names I'd relinquished twenty-five jazz albums
Not soda pop caps, not rebus puzzles, not loopy strips
An apparatchik from agriculture came in — Aleksandr slipped
    his filchings aside — blood of my blood and flesh of my
    flesh I am a worker — I don't know how the hard
    currency found its way into the case for my eye glasses
The general said he understood everything — there would be
    no further panzer costs taken from the colonel's pay
Perhaps his mind deserved a better time and place
Speaking Engels in the living room from the sofa
A film showing the kid with the bomb
People floating in the winter light above the ice — on light

Chapter Twenty-Six

I was asked to explain the phrase sex kitten and the term pussy
Gray sky, frost crushed on trees
The light lifted in the Vyborg district, people floating past on
ice
Shown by incident
Writings blown from nationalists — they lacked the syllables of
    spy
I've fully supplied my own body's place in society, Arkadii said
Not dust, not task, not statuesque
And love of pets, which has no efficacy? he asked — language
    itself is partially love but of another kind
Two crows rose out of a tiny park as if lifted by a swarm of
    other birds
I arranged myself in explication — slowly lifting my right arm
A pose knowing that it can be allowed
It was absurd — like thoughts around the edge of what needs
    to be understood
He deferred
He asked which women prefer

Chapter Twenty-Seven

Over the years I have conspired — many plots resulting in no
    U.S.-Soviet anthologies
I've smelled the cabbage — to prepare the salad you crush it in
    your hands
I've smelled the wet, the bed — the conspiratorial tone and leg
    and wool blanket
Lyosha was at the upright machine
Lenin had slept on the bed
So why have they been whispering, I asked in Ilya's ear
It's about paper, he said — we wonder how much paper a San
    Francisco-St. Petersburg anthology would be allowed
Boris came in, made formal greetings, and sat down beside me
    on the edge of the bed
We have no hands for competition, he said, but for
    composition we have many heads
Outside the window beside the Griboyedova canal a man was
    fishing for a carton of cigarettes bobbing just beyond his
    butterfly net on a belt
We are cerebral
If he would just cross the bridge he could reach them
Let's think of nature as distinct from industry, of romanticism
    in distance and wit
Such is our witticism, while on the far side of the canal a group
    of adolescent boys appeared and, hardly stopping, still
    shouting, they dropped some chunks of broken concrete
    into the canal to make the waves which washed the carton
    back within reach of the man

Chapter Twenty-Eight

One guy sits beside a famous river
Another guy digs an irrigation canal
Such is allegory
And metaphor! — it is a great packer
A chemical
So what then did you see and do in Leningrad
Can you answer my riddle
If you ask it
The child of my father but not me — who is it
A point of no return — a moment of denunciation
The colonel's wife picked up the kettle and added water to the
    tea
They don't know and neither do I, she said
He took a butter-bread
Of course!—the brother of the cab driver

Chapter Twenty-Nine

An exhortation and I've slept
I must be addressed — I'm one of the tools of my trade
But I beg myself not to offer any explanations
Stories
Birds
The stores have a little bit of rice in them
The babies are left by their shoppers in the sun near the door
Everything else is real
The faces very familiar — though they wear expressions I'd
    never have understood
We are hunters, not kidnappers, Zina said
And this could go on without me — every child becoming
    human
A guard, a mushroom hunter, a someone — slogging
A person puts a pillow to its mindfulness
More night

Chapter Thirty

It's somewhere to be hasty from, to await a meal
The mail never comes
There's moisture on the wall which seals the wallpaper
So I'm gaping at the paintings there (Timur's, Afrika's,
    Ostap's) from the interior of a bed
You cannot touch me on my papers
In such a language, so I said
The region sings under a stack
Then the rustling or pluckle of rain
I'm preparing a translation of *Xenia*
Some old rags are greasily burning
Two children with a sled are playing silently on the neon-
    yellow ice
There is something embarrassing about nature's power
It's part of nature's routine
Can one prepare for history

Chapter Thirty-One

We had taken pleasure in efficacy
Nature offers efficacy and devours pleasure
But it is trivial that I have to sleep beside an open window
Yet Zina too
We prepared within a few minutes of each other
From the sofa we spoke of the written sentence, from the
    kitchen of prison
On which side of the guard is the word
And so forth
Alarming symbols are everywhere
And so the family is divided
Gavronsky is a wonder or a thug
And here we are, said Arkadii, beside the Moika paddling to
    our throats in filthy blood
So we actually argued — I was furious that he didn't know my
    violence, he was enraged that I didn't admit his
We love to feed our pleasure to nature, I said

Chapter Thirty-Two

I haven't been conscious of inadmissibility
It's like snow in the angles of ovals
And the question of the necessity of art isn't the subject of my
    novel
Necessity isn't any more abstract than beauty, Anna said — it's
    all subjective
So, Papa, added Ostap, how could it be good and anyway —
    why not bad
No, no, said Gavronsky — maybe she's right and art is
    political — but I don't see how you can know which side
    of politics it's on
On application
Soviet painting to Soviet medicine
The fascination of the big thing
The fear of the hole in the yellow arm
The thing about
We have a deeply unpleasant sense of our animal nature
There are blue jaws moving over the bare white trees
We are keeping up with our manifestos, he said, but we always
    add our dismay

Chapter Thirty-Three

Perhaps there's a foray of ghost before life
The devil appeared, Salik said, and told Salik that he can't fly
He flies
He is flying over the place where he will spend — or did
    spend — much of his childhood and he wants to descend
    but the quality of his flying is so strong that he can't leave
    the sky
Then he recognizes his mother — she's standing in the
    sunlight and he lands
All around the airport naively blocking traffic are such boys
    recruited from Uzbekistan
As merry as life's sky in which rise bulls-eyes
A loss of self with a high level of content
One day Salik's mother tells him to go back to the hills to fly
On his way, Salik said, he met the devil again
And again the devil tells him he can't fly
This time he's right
Salik can't fly — his shadow binds him to Uzbekistan
But when he's transparent, the devil says, Salik will fly again

Chapter Thirty-Four

The wind would take care of it
You could see it was a street without a tongue
And I should leave my shoes by the door
But we went for cheese and then tapochki
The flesh partially blinded, sharing space
The flesh prevents the sweeping of a large society
The muffle could take forever
But what a coincidence it is with my objectivity to sleep
Poetry is compressed according to one scale and prose
        according to another
Viktor said so, leaning — these matters are temporal
Sleepily
The whole skull a wet window
The film of droplets envelops solitude
Laborious, ballooning, and practical

Chapter Thirty-Five

The colonel's daughter was scraping circles on the trolley
    window in enormous frost
The kagebeshnik asked us
Ice, endurance — ice
But we weren't from Florida
And the colonel had requested and now insisted that his
    daughter stop
But amaze, amazed — we must excuse
The public morality is completely apart from the rampant
    inspection of frost
Lifting frost
Swirling ice of ashes and frost
Papa, why should saying that make me stop — every day you
    ignore Mama saying again don't you piss in the kitchen
    sink tonight
Drifting tender frost
Confusing crime and nationalism, the guy is a shifting
    defender
Through the circle she scraped something skeletal
It covered only the surface of something as banalities overlie

Chapter Thirty-Six

At the next stop the door fell off
I was to remember but not to mind
But as not mine, whose — a paradise possessionless
A sky of particles transpires
Disassembled, with the vagueness of humility — but it's
    disinterest bobbing
And pressing
To the metallic foretaste of Leningrad's mineral water
Proportions, memories, infinities, trolleys — all the forms of
    weariness that guide us, Dima said, through the otherness
    of tangibility
Through holes
There's no unconscious space in the mind, Viktor said
I relaxed, was at peace
Life sufficed
It was an inactive comedy in its yellow Leningrad day
Its mineral lifting

Chapter Thirty-Seven

The effective life of a bald man on a motorcycle bearing an
    accordion churns up the red soil and fans the sky
We escalated into the metro from there
A babushka was riding below balancing a great new porcelain
    washtub
The solid egg on chicken legs
The hammer destroying the tablecloth, the transition
The table worsening, then the littlest chair
A cabbage must be milked
But the finger was clumsily knicked instead — I tried to hide it
    with a thumb
No touch now unless I touch
Empty heat in the hard currency store
A new abstraction — a new Rilke
We have had our resolution
Dive, flight, and then wrest
Ostap pointed toward a slab of frying spam and said, that
    organism is what we call fruit

Chapter Thirty-Eight

Some were the days — days confessed — for the unofficial show
Gavronsky departed from his overcoat and blushed
Ears so sweet at the door, some whispered
Sustained pedagogy
Then the painters left — they were wearing coats but their
    chests were bare — to the Architects Union on Gertsena
    where the restaurant would be open
It is impossible to imagine a painter more different than his
    grandfather
Go back at once, a hoarse voice called
It was bored and not inclined to read
It was a summer consumed by a worm
Those are the Semite cat's words, the hoarse anti-Semite voice
    called
Memory called
Not pornographic, Gavronsky said, and not political
An architect passed the door with a platter of sturgeon and
    black mushrooms
Not painting, said Gavronsky — worse

Chapter Thirty-Nine

Neither art nor life is opposite
Opposition is a stupid government in power to misunderstand
The grandmother prided herself on her ability to count
      backward as fast and as far as forward
Another woman further up the stairs thought perhaps she
      didn't understand something but actually she didn't
      believe in something
She wants, she said, to prepare for a social reality, one that
      politics could predict, that kindness could guarantee
The vehement grandmother was preparing her place in it
But what of the intolerable bathos of the colonel
The washtub slipped
Momentous shift
This was a crime in life now substantiated by a crime in art
A nationalist was going by a guise — the same quivering
The washtub idle lightened sped
Items rise, ripen, and must fall
The washtub overtook the colonel

Chapter Forty

Siberia begins again, Dima said, fifteen minutes from
    Leningrad
The conversations held in a range, pressed in descent
But with a terrible clatter and outbreaks of melancholy
Wistfully Kolya had actually said, now we have freedom without
    oppression but freedom with oppression had strength and
    this freedom is almost dead
People are reciting Pushkin like hyenas again
Freedom, tea, and beatitude
Arkadii's grandmother had run it over his body and then
    sucked out the egg
Thrown into the tub the colonel descended the metro
    escalator like a child in winter over melting and
    insufficient snow down a stony mountain hillside on a sled
I knew what you name, I name what you saw
An adept in a lifetime at these mysteries fills itself with what's
    on just fifteen of those pages
The old writer drops to the floor to sit on just one
We are tucked in loss
We are wrapped in greasy pages, in the porous snow of eyes
At the foot of the escalator from the porcelain washtub the
    colonel turns as he rises

Chapter Forty-One

Crows at the dog's eyes swinging her building
Such a person as a writer not only may but must appear
Solicitude had for several days now developed a theory, a
    polemic
I have not isolated the active element of my medium — my
    medium is mediation
Aesthetic impression swimming clockwise
The eyes and cheeks of hate
An angel's violent ways
An enormous force passes through — we want urgently to
    know what changes
The gray of a fish
A drunk moaning on Nekrasova, embracing a lamppost, legs
    like wet pillars in clumsy felt boots, begging us to break
    open the lamppost and release him
Crazy — he has a monstrous fascination for a big thing, says a
    passerby who stops to ask us for a match
Is it an actual object of contemplation
The colonel has aimed, the old woman falls — why not — her
    porcelain tub had crumpled his epaulets
An amazing tub — she must have hunted for days to find it

Chapter Forty-Two

Snow later — we came by a back door into the Architects
    Union cafe and the snow progressed
If you count your money, you limit it
But reality is the matter mediated
Sad, unchanged
The intermediate
Now see there but when where
No future, no past
I think Grisha is in a mafia
Absolutely, Ilya said, not
Just the pastel green of an unclocked solitude
Snow to obtain a result of frost roses
Of shock — but a terrible scream burst in the room
And then an explosion (we would be scaled to the
    phenomenology of this violence) — in eleven sounds — it
    was only Gavronsky who didn't hear the knife
Gavronsky with its mouth

Chapter Forty-Three

He saw something, he felt something
He loved, he saw pink snow, he smelled the enemy
Speech
Crows in a winter mimic
Our comments fall into different semantics
By turns, they are philosophical, anecdotal, and intimate
Our experiences achieve pathos when they force us to
    acknowledge that the significances and meanings of
    things — things we've known, it would seem, forever, and
    certainly since early childhood — have changed — or
    rather, when we are forced to absorb the memory of being
    utterly unable to catch or trace or name the moment of
    transition when one meaning changed to another — the
    moment of interruption in the course of our knowing
    such things
It was a kind of bed in the yellowish blood of Gavronsky
And now the sun is so bright on the street that it seems to
    shatter everything — the shops in the neighborhood are
    in splinters, fragments of cars fly by, arms and legs flail
    along the sidewalk, shards of colored stucco catapult past
    my face, blue rags flutter in my peripheral vision — my
    myopia has increased and the wind blows my hair in my
    eyes
Poetry is violent
The meanings of the words annihilate each other, Arkadii said
In this sense all the acts of the Marquis de Sade imitate writing
But women are not afraid
When we've lured a man, when we see him in the distance,
    we'll scatter, my dears — we'll bomb him with cherries

Chapter Forty-Four

It's not a panzer tank but the colonel's mistress
Drinking and late in the kitchen
Faint — using an infinitive to express necessity
Of necessity immobile, flickering, in sex, pressed
Writers work with small signs — so small they persist
But there's always some teacher lecturing endlessly from his
    collapsing podium with an infinite text
The main creative goal of the painter is to run away from this
    teacher
On Gertsena where Gavronsky lay awkward guys in boots were
    pretending to investigate
They continued to indulge in childish conceptualism,
    inventing folklore from crosswords and games
But Gavronsky grew fainter, scarcely seething
The real operative police work with the air and they discover
    there a lot of things
An observer and the scene observed in an egg
Across the street were Nabokov's windows
Then the ambulance arrived from the urgent ward

Chapter Forty-Five

All tender winds are foreseen tunes
Arkadii adjusted smokes
You have a word for the clear ice that flows like a mirror after
    thaws on the window glass
The yellow goes blue between
Clinging frost and oil
They are irritating coffee
They are spreading speed with nails
There is a third principle, said Borya, and it's compression
Poetry anticipates a love of thinking
Yes, but also the mobility of experience
Untargeted experience
Katya had been on Gertsena — some complications of
    intention
But the attack on Gavronsky — no one could say yet if the
    nationalist had sought whom he stabbed
Katya called to say Gavronsky had muttered that like Trotsky
    he would die for three days

Chapter Forty-Six

I tipped my shoulder and it poured, the painter said
There was no rehearsal, only the big show, the shirt soaked
Its participants for many years to sustain in the exogamic
    culture
What have you in common
At home in the Spartan nudity
It's funny to call it cold, Arkadii said
The incident resulted in a privileged titillation
Patience, elongation, exacerbated gratitude, and a desire to be
    a doctor
So, there is a difference between masculine and feminine
    hedonism
For some space is more nude than astonishment
And women's powers of resilience are prestigious
It's very competitive to be submissive
I accomplished several great submissions
Stripped

Chapter Forty-Seven

The poem is protracted in evidence
With the poem's protection
Through a woods (just beyond the housing block) or from
 female faces showing stopping places
The poem's thing is printless, Arkadii said — but I don't know
 so
The poem perturbed — any idiot can implore
A small part of the panzer deplored by the wife
I probed with my fork — all fish and bones
A stone in a great stretch of clothing
The neighbor on his narrow balcony was stroking his dog on a
 crust of snow
There's a kind of swamp above and below mosquitoes
The shadow of that mosquito is the cloud
In two meters between sofa and stove dripping clothes
Persons feeding themselves in the steady sense
A sturdy exit from paradise

Chapter Forty-Eight

In spite of appearances — those intervals denounced —
    (namely futilities) — the banners are down
The samovar stood on a tackle
In the hotel room the television stood unplugged too far on a
    table from the outlet to work and the table so fragile that
    to move it would collapse it
It had been my humor to protect it
This we have in common
One-inch squares of pasta, a one-hour tour of Pavlovsk
And people feeding ducks
The seductive winter weather germinated breadcrumbs and
    old men, women, children, fathers, kagebeshniks,
    apparatchiks, tourists, buryats, nationalists, hooligans,
    cossacks, and journalists to toss them
With every toss a tiny blast
Do we invite these ducks or do we claim them
We offer ourselves in our untemporal motherhoods
In the old yellow neighborhood with the free enterprise
    garage for tire montage
Feeding the ducks constructs our absence
Hence one-meter squares of fabric for porous visual fields
    folded, tucked in pocket

Chapter Forty-Nine

Listened to gunfire — what is it?
A blow it was, again — who is guilty?
All empires have put my ego to slumber and thence to
    slaughter
Death is recited to laughter
A youth from the Crimea
He is lying on his back very relaxed when I ask
Yes, he says, I am so sweet, stabilized, with such solidarity
In Lvov in the beer factory there are drinking rats
And one rat lies on her back holding an egg in her paws
    against her stomach while another takes her by the tail
    and drags her away
Real winter over the couch weather longing
In the bathroom the spigot over the sink swinging pours into
    the tub
Intent, purpose, and resource
The man unperturbed in the next room shot upward in the
    shower
The poor peltering subsides

Chapter Fifty

I said to myself that the fever was refunding
Universal women in a coupon economy
An American adds that Leningrad's a city of women
There's no exit to objectivity
But of course women know what they want
Their figure in a nose
A chair firmly set on the ground reserved
They have speakable satisfactions
Snows
Snow flies on their eyes
Their weight is rewarded
Their children seize it with trembling hands
They are fully capable of a bodily need
There is no call to demonstrate the experience

Chapter Fifty-One

It would be inexcusable to stop
There's a city of disintegrations
A pipe in Pushkin's house has popped, it sings
The water drops
A student shudders
Some fixed or heavy object strikes my stride
Some loose objective, its likes and dislikes
I started violently—but tenderly
Briefly, at pains, in the light, wind and limb, true participants
But such a brilliant gulf, with two men in high boots sweeping
    it, and in the distance the Swedish hotel, Mitya's flat, the
    old clock, Olya's desk, the dirty sheets, and Seryozha
    singing in falsetto
Maybe it's impossible — dilemmas floating a regime
Lenin's finger at Finland — the revolution was not pedantic
Outside Arkadii's thumb stands a small tattoo
A blue bamboo

Chapter Fifty-Two

It's Armenian at all that someone has faith in your wealth
Fear of telling in America for its money authority
No night falling
And a little girl was playing on Vasilii Island between the
    switching rails where Malii Prospekt meets Nalichnaya
    Street
Every night the ghosts become more numerous and violent
Their special interest is in altered states of consciousness and
    speech
The rails switched and seized one of her feet
There was a colonel across the metal
It is futile, he said later, to fight against your feet
The colonel was just crossing the street
A man at a window was thinking in his writing light
A life locked in that look — the colonel with the child
Behind her a trolley turned the corner toward them —
    speeding in gray light, it was now almost night
The child and the colonel continued their fight

Chapter Fifty-Three

At any second one can refuse lack of feeling and find it
Thoughtless, constituent
This is an inevitable time of accumulation, of calm
I was in the proximity of my own persistence and in itself
    untraceable
The usual (suspect in itself) blink of suspicion
But you must know why you are in Leningrad, said Vodonoy
In a metonym
It's not displacement but relocation
In fact on the same date we were doing both sleeping and
    waking
Preoccupied with production, always provided with basic
    necessities, a person like itself
Listening to the ringing of the other sides of streets
As a woman's baby one napped by poppies in the Ukraine
Repeating, dispersed, tired
The excitation of the same experience by two grammars — it's
    not impossible

Chapter Fifty-Four

A 5, maybe a 42

The trolley

The colonel himself the maneuver his brain would run

All aspects of the Army are to be represented, even a Jewish
barber

There will be a bronze tree with places in the branches for 50
birds

Of course a fragment of the Kremlin wall will be included

At the front of the monument will be many figures, some
attacking, some kissing the red banner, some hammering,
shoveling — everyone doing something

At the center is a great figure of a woman standing on a vast
globe

The motherland

The fat snake of fascism has risen and bites at her

In one hand, the right one, she has seized a shield — her
sword leans against the tree

Small men are hacking at the snake with knives

Shield in the right hand — she can't take her sword — in her
left hand lies the pigeon of peace

The colonel has pulled off his overcoat and covered the child

Chapter Fifty-Five

So much have yet to be postsentiments
You lose hypothesis, as Gavronsky said
The experience was all matrix
So it was impossible to distinguish ghosts from guests
It's strange work — to search for regularities
In the next room was a goldfish swimming counterclockwise in
     a round glass bowl over the half skull of a human
Something from which I should protect my child — her name
     was Mira Rabotnaya
One dreams in retrospection
My dreams were a different Russia
The sound made at the front of the mouth
The blindness which is behind sight
The dog in the desert who met a man's eyes
Arkadii pressed his tongue to the roof of his mouth, clacked,
     and Zina opened the window and looked down
We were clocked and came precisely as due

Chapter Fifty-Six

The child was blinded by the greatcoat to die
Not agent nor agency but instrument
The idea is to preserve from the sight of what serves
The canal but no potential
The bare statues in the Summer Garden boxed to spare them
    from the lifting frost
Behind closed windows through open curtains the neighbor was
    dancing with his collie on its hindlegs
The old woman's husband hit the nail in her head
The toddler was lost in a communal flat by going to sleep in what
    he saw was a darker drawer
It was his dilemma to sleep
It was his dilemma to say he was paying for a panzer
Another colonel knew all along — such poetry isn't beauty, it's
    inquiry
We have any experience to deliberate
In sex inquiry
At the door stood her legs and boots

Chapter Fifty-Seven

The mosquitoes were sleeping in the cellar for the winter
Inspiration in abeyance, no sense of mind
No sense of life size
Is sex the excess of subjectivity
Everything happens so frequently there's no sense in saying so
So even in the enormous space of a New York loft you can
    instantly find your own glass, Gavronsky said
Gavronsky was explaining his theory of the tiny sign
Progress suspended, no condition to maintain
Persons find themselves increasingly small in this century, so
    that smaller and smaller things appear normal
If Leonardo were to paint La Gioconda today he'd put her in a
    3-inch square
The jiggling of all things 30 to 40 centimeters high — no more
Sex the excess of objectivity
It seemed to be cold, but it might have been wet
Zero degrees celsius — no less

Chapter Fifty-Eight

Some possibilities take place on a plate
A process whose pace doesn't coincide with comprehension's
    pace
I remember the instructions
To see is such deferred
Zina was jarring the milky liquid for Ostap's priming
Such is our medicine, he said
Old people's skulls thicken
I am to interrupt myself tonight at exactly 8 and propose a
    toast to "our colleagues who at this moment are reading
    verses in Tambov"
Both largeness and lozenge to collide
The crows voices in winter light like copper pliers
The reading an open word shutter
Only slats, and they faded into winter
Paints (of any color), aspirin, artichoke hearts, and printer
    ribbon
Dispersal at either end — eight passed without interruption

Chapter Fifty-Nine

If you whistle a tune within a flat its residents will never have
    cash
The collie was barking on the opposite balcony it filled above
    the trees with its inexhaustible faculty of negation
It puts grammar to the hunt
Ducks swimming in the black backwash of the canal and
    several women and children feeding them in the wind
It isn't the cold — scarcely one degree of frost — but the wind
    increases the sensation of it
The feeding of everyday life put to sex
I like such gaps, Arkadii said
A neighborhood of rotting bricks housing an enterprise of
    brick
In the next neighborhood a plant of plasticity
And wind — Zina tightened my hood
The ground emitted an odor of tin
No clocks worked
From the sensual instability of volition, of willfulness, of
    intention I had slept
I was not disappointed

Chapter Sixty

He was not nationalist, Vasya said
The room was blue, the hue an indescribable grasp
It was not village prose and not a Siberian correction
Misha was moaning with hangover
There was honey on the dish and three spoons
They have made him write a trilogy and then they dispensed
There was humiliation in its typing
It was a great joke
Then what is prophesy but a logical violation
A sort of limerick, but longer
A mechanic, and more fortunate
A Soviet Faulkner, a Soviet Rilke
There are constant predicates and variable subjects
One smokes in a bog and eats leather, the other's trailing the
        sun on the street

Chapter Sixty-One

A ram has a job — interruptions, just leaping
Sleeping past the depression that reality divides
It's assigned to lead the other rams and sheep to slaughter
Perhaps the traveller should be obsequious, not the one who
    resides
Sleeping between itself and not-itself
The cousin to a navy guy, just up for adoption
The corpses behind and the ram ahead
One day it takes a stand and refuses to do so
If there are no great opposites there are no great parallels
In the film Alyosha described the ram is condemned then and
    itself is slaughtered
Another ram takes over the job — it simply replaces it
There are many Bambis, Bambi is normal
A face so familiar and one sees that it expresses something in
    life that we have seen on that face
Alone, after work, things were happening to it

Chapter Sixty-Two

If each day were new a person would be incomprehensible
To misunderstand it was to be rejected
The person left out, in its unSoviet sensation
Many things left in observation
Greeting a man we pretend is a man we've come to meet, we
    were admitted into the Writers Union
Black mushrooms stuffed in sturgeon, radishes, vodka — the
    sturgeon rolled and sealed
The oak was very complicated — Masonic groves, the grooves
    in plots, and Jews
There are members of memory and they have attacked the
    Jews
Jamal talked of race cars and wood carvings
I had run far faster than any of the other white girls could do
Or of confinement and submission
Something further had to be said about a cousin, a forger, in
    prison
Every man to his mafia, Feodor said
To America

Chapter Sixty-Three

Goodbye, America, which I have never seen
I float forever in my paper boat
A paper flicker, no telephone
If there would be phone, there would be love
No taken distance — but there's only difference
Description of it is a form of waiting
But the time deteriorates
I remember how it was, and what a fine memory of it was
    forming
Or that was the anticipation
Cold was imminent and my sense of it merely deferred
The climate was inexact and inert
With the person disappeared the person's obsequiousness
The person now morose or immune
It's afloat in its intimations

Chapter Sixty-Four

It takes days to give spring the appearance of pregnancy
Laid out under incense on unwashed ice
The belly absorbing increments of bed
This irritation changes life into a sequence of time lapses
Its fathers witty, optimistic, in lips
Its mothers witnessed, as great as limbo
Then one day a completely by-the-way and nonobligatory
    sound occurs, a mumbling as of wasps or sheep
Sincere amazement — there are real holes in the wall
    reflecting light so that they appear lemon ocher
In one there are two men, in that rigid state of sociability
    wherein conditions common to the lives of both of them
    have militarized them momentarily — Americans
And they feel themselves, or some particle of themselves, to be
    a formidable force against the world, not denying reality
    but on the contrary facing it
And there is only reality
One is supporting an enormous domino, the double three,
    and the other supports his own arm and hand with his
    elbow resting on the red table beside the erect rectangle
I said that a fly had appeared in the operating room
It sat like a crystal of black salt on the bed

Chapter Sixty-Five

A question occurred about *Opoyaz*
The so-called mathematical approach
Empty stores
The satchel of Lydia Yakovlevna on psychological prose
There's such impertinence in subjectivity
But what could one predict from the syntax of a desire to
    surpass the opposition between "me" and "you"
Some manifestation of life as a whole
Old-style trolleys passed through the Vyborg, but taken in mist
    they had disappeared
Jugs of muddy juice, half settled pulp, remained in plenitude
In web
Bourgeois lyricism is predictable, Papa, said Ostap — there'd
    been a necrorealist film called "The Hydroelectric Leg"
They very frequently said names — Mitya, Vitya —active
    repetitions
At dusk in the Vyborg the colonel, sweating under his fur hat,
    was making his way through the park on the darkening
    snow to the thawing path
Our colonel in sum total

Chapter Sixty-Six

The ridiculous cemetery was full of birds
Shadows stood to the stone sun
Transcendence explains time no more than paint explains
    space
The speck, the curve — prediction
Prediction and its charity keep us dying
Prediction and its collage
Dostoevsky would have put it under glass inside a frame
Gogol would have marked it with a promise that reality will
    settle like frost
Don't trust yourself, I write for you, and so forth
Form subjugates every experience
Thus a man lost his bag between the doors of the bus as the
    bus drove away when we ourselves had just jumped on it
Some looking back and some running forward
Someone leaned over two old women holding boxes and
    jerked up the window, passengers passed the tattered bag,
    someone pushed the bag out the window — the bus
    turned a corner, potatoes and carrots spilled, and the
    man appeared
The absurd occurrence could come between suns

Chapter Sixty-Seven

The father of my cousin had his mouth around the doorknob
The universe unframed
Shoes removed at the door
We socked communicants without authorship of scene
Our language was divided into states of line
But such is the theater of hospitality
The hostess experiencing the pleasure of pleasure
The music is set in the red plastic player after rubbing some
        grease off one knob
The presence of the third person is critical — it being a
        description — taking the satisfaction of being greeted
The third and first persons exchanged images in the makeshift
        intimacy of the cluttered room
A painting of John Lennon was framed behind the glass front
Of Bunin pursuing sequential moments in the thinking
        process
The human figure becomes increasingly abstract as it grows
        older
It is weight not hinge

Chapter Sixty-Eight

This person was a writer of notorious interruptions
I found real pleasure in this patience, more than I took
And I felt how weak my unsettling legs were becoming — two
    legs synonymous in their vagueness
It was a real banquet table
Nights and link — but I think in threes
Such emotion is never absent
A woman wants to slice onions
And carrots near black
But in ribbons or in lozenges
Blood on cabbage
In the pocket of the bag were some strands from Yalta
I described its vacationers, replications, perspiring players
Interruptions wouldn't constitute a parade
Too little time, so one regrets whatever one doesn't

Chapter Sixty-Nine

I had a theory of sleep and of prose and of sausage buried in
    forest
I kept them distinct
The 600 seconds had fallen silent
The television is a turtle, not a beetle, I said, in a shell with the
    gift of speech
The mere mood of our words was producing content
The sheer detail was required
Sleep is an orientation
There's no need to distinguish a poem from prose
It will not let you be completely submerged in the drowsing of
    a great long-distance
Arkadii, said Vitya, writes his novel to eliminate illiteracy
He is frenzied by all this phenomenology
It makes him indignant
I don't agree, Arkadii said, it has no cause
A great cobweb taken out of position

Chapter Seventy

A woman in feather in a landscape of squares
Gavronskaya had lounged in comic theater
Useful works, sought by science, past truckloads of frosted
    cabbage
A literary theater presents the spatial distribution of things
An agoraphobia that glitters, a canvas cut to torso, the toe
    sucked and nothing diminished
Since glasnost it was a personal press
And there were impressions of the attack on a strip of film
    made and mailed anonymously
It was no longer than the blade of a butterfly knife
"This author, deeply disturbed by recent impulses" and so
    forth
The ruble is a poor metonym for Leningrad
The use of a word is no metonym for time
Gavronsky within his chest bound from the hospital
Eros, erosion — only bread, drinking in bed
Each time in webs

Book Two

Chapter Seventy-One: Truth

Truth is not precision but evidence
Body and truth at the thought
Crazy who says no longer and is quickly repeated
To hover and hum at the truth (so much longer to love)
To hush
Over ground under cloud as expedient as expands
Nothing had — no moral outrage, no self-righteousness, no
    indignation
Just residue
An all-over corporeal stamina
There isn't really room for truth — gray birches in full
context — but room for both
As always, as ambient, and as bound
Just as blue, the procedure, reflects
The truth that is halted is squandered
Even the lull is dependent

Chapter Seventy-Two: Nature

The frost falls from a tree
We have a state of nature
Maybe I need the tree — it will acknowledge and thereby
    authorize me
Nature as describer — with the Russian names for things
Nature, which I regard across the table of which it's the
    proprietor
It is the third (inhuman) person
Waning interest, sugar rationing, a thumb before the moon
    without hypocrisy
The natural part of that thought is from a dream
I in my progress passing this
A hunter is in its artlessness
Nature results in the lack of privacy (personality) that would
    go with it
It pursues the impersonal narrative — here, our endless it
So I was feeling an inferior weariness, an inability to
    acknowledge anything
It was snowing, and the snow was rippled by the people
    walking in it while at the same time the people were
    reflected in it

Chapter Seventy-Three: Innocence

I was afraid to look — two men overheard in the dark were
    speaking of prison
I wasn't innocent, though I meant to be
An ant travelled to the end of each pubic hair
The colonel's coat was guarding the trolley's innocence
One man said he remembered as a boy climbing through a
    gap in a fence
Language was needed there for understanding, not for speech
Eventually everything turns back and it's voluptuous to repeat
The thin white rim of the hole reflects the black light of the
    lamp
One falls through that hole in memory
Vasya remembered looking through that hole in 1935 but only
    one time and seeing that the ground on the other side
    was heaving as "enemies" died
Innocence sustaining
Stains of splattered cherries in the stairwell — throat
Rain — the window shut
It all originates in a mistaken sighting

Chapter Seventy-Four: Conspiracy

Here — there's a feeling of snow near the eyes
Two suns would form
A basket of nothing — hieroglyphic
In those circles conspiracies were not fastidious
They told everything — how many fish heads resulted, where
    the poison-green flowers of lightning had shook, the exact
    (and still evident) moment the Bulgarian clock broke
Every glint was bulging
There were intricacies covering such authenticity
And why not — it came down to the anecdote and then rose
    again
Pragmatism recounted
Over and over — there is conspiracy in repetition
Windings in what dissipates
A conspiracy is made within resistance to distraction
They had no secrets — they were lost in the comparison
Highly significant, filled with sense, centrifugal symbols swirled

Chapter Seventy-Five: Passion

Passion is the alienation that love provides
Drifting winter tinted where we lifted, plowed
Jealousy is a flake of a different passion
It was hungry to be plunging in disruption
The wobble and mattering of the sensing muscles which
    combine
People are not joined in passion but divulged
They diverge — but that sight was unseen
But all this is muffled in banalities, I said
It is not passion to nod in
It is passion for no one to listen
One with closed eyes and the other one's opened
The snowfall offered all the colors of apple
There was passion in its thud and exhilaration
Patience itself pushes over — given a body for what

Chapter Seventy-Six: Design

Pushkin's body had apparent lively symmetry
Or someone's intellectual resource prematurely
Poor body — every person is somewhat designed
It drew up — each bus a blossom on the tangled bus vines
There were so many places in which we didn't sit that where
    we did seemed, well, preordained or little used
We rode in time like rhymes and counted stops to Gorky
Gavronsky was rubbed by egg, Gavronskaya sucked through
    the shell, and Pushkin died
Pushkin designed — with pressure
We oscillated toward the city center and later back again
Pushkin lay naked in his room on the rug writing in solitude or
    visiting with friends
The breath and body heat of Pushkin steamed
The fog on the windows gleamed — dripped
It was design but without climb
We jumped from the sweating bus — there were clusters of
    buildings in every direction numbered without sequence
    but after a time we sorted them out and arrived at Sasha's
    with our bottles of wine

Chapter Seventy-Seven: Suffering

A stench left from cooking fish lay frenzied, fell inert
Or a yellow rose frustrated in the Summer Garden
Mayakovsky said that horses never commit suicide because they
    don't know how to talk — they could never explain their
    suffering
Each night has wiped a suffering diagonally — in such
    conditions each voice and face becomes distorted
From a neighboring building an infant has been crying for five
    hours
With seething or mellifluous endurance — Arkadii said
    nothing could be recognized
A seep in suffering — loss is different
Sight gone, blood poisoned, sleepless, anonymous along the
    street
Along the bottom of the foot dogs barked, a pendulum swung
Or the pendulum tossed
Now the next generation is suffering, Tynianov told Shklovsky;
    we turned out to be poor nourishment and they are bad
    eaters
Each suffering adds to the unrecognizable
The time has arrived
Night, interrupted, follows another night

Chapter Seventy-Eight: Betrayal

There were wives to follow the Decembrists, among them
    Pushkin lovers
To a Siberia of sex? a cold of poetry?
And no betrayal nor clarity for sex — he might then have been
    a bottle
That is an interest — betraying logic at any level
Someone in camouflage rasps out a prison song
But how could he travel?
Imperfect openings — they are reflections
Betrayal is a kind of mirror (art is not)
One colonel betrayed the other, but within mere weeks they
    were just two indistinguishable fellows, twins reflected in
    the mud
At enmity while at empathy
Total disappearance is the goal of each activity
We have abandoned our fidelity to big things, Olya explained
But in small we don't betray
The fact itself comes to its limits, in its visits, of which we speak
    in words having nothing in common with the fact of its
    existence

Chapter Seventy-Nine: Death

The back of the head waits for death
The feeling of weakness, a gentle indifference
The tree of language sheds too much foliage
It is death to be without shadow
Each head is a mound — the case is empty
What is it thinking? — but it can't be thinking
It had no difference
It must be by itself — I'm slightly terrified
Someone was embracing the air above it
And it's virtually invisible to me, my bulge above the nape
It can't speak — and yet it greets you
It keeps no memories
I would like to believe it, but it's the same as waiting
Why not have waited

Chapter Eighty: Redemption

Two rams, which ram redeemed
One ram wasted, one ram waiting
Maybe the same ram — in romance wandering
In descriptions crossing and saw things
Barges hardly higher than the surface of the water bore meat
    bones slipping under the bridges
At two a.m. the bridges rose for bigger boats, then fell at 4:55,
    and rose at five again
We sped across — the Lada rammed through the falling snow
The trees shook, atoning for momentum
Where we say "he's a crook" they say "he's a corner"
The notorious Russian soul, fulfilling our goal
We were laughing at the Russian novel
We will say, the slower you go the farther you'll get and plain
    water is glad to get a crow
We will be redeemed, we will be rescued
We will believe everything we say

Book Three

Chapter Eighty-One

Leningrad lies in the haze of its sides
It lies as a heroine
Now it is both
How not — the not is sometimes impossible to reach
It was
But then is the work of art not an act but an object of memory
Then from a great disturbance
The most delicate message accumulates
But you must know why you write a novel, saidVodonoy
It's not to displace anything
It has context and metronome
By insisting on a comprehension of every word I am free to
    signify place though not to represent it
So I must oppose the opposition of poetry to prose
Just as we can only momentarily oppose control to
discontinuity, sex to organization, disorientation to domestic
    time and space, and glasnost (information) to the hunt

Chapter Eighty-Two

A crow was grunting in the snow
But what's the difference — every text aims at the complete
    realization of one's self-unimportance
A paradise
How could we ever finish what we never started
Zina, I said
Ho
What is it called
Freud's Meeting with a Cossack Mama
Zina's blankets were replaced by Tanya's
Youth is a situation of designations
Assonance and repetition slow language and emphasize labor
Last year's new foliage was a silverish fog of green
This year's will be also
The narrative tense in a future one — experience is an object
    of memory

Chapter Eighty-Three

Experience is only indirectly responsible for words
Rumbling snow
The window is sound
But words must have the experience of it
Licking at the world, ogling, eavesdropping apples
The colonel's wife said her mother's heart told her a terrible
    thing
Then at two in the morning the doorbell rang
This-worldly, laborious, elliptical
Just the daughter's two legs in a pair of soldier's boots standing
on a note which said, "Mama, I'm home"
They prevent their face
At dawn ants overran the snow
An inexhaustible thaw spread with their impatience
The legs are columns of itch
Our exhaustion might account for the passage of time but not
    for progress through it, through innumerable temporal
    passages or conduits without a subsequent sense of
    communication, of acknowledgment, and of achievement

Chapter Eighty-Four

Ostap said the old woman was still shouting that the bastard
    had nailed it in
Zina was boring the rot from a peeled potato
Later I experienced the memory of an enormous expectation
    of happiness
The rest of the world is independent
The ear muffs of its fur hat are turned down and its nose is
    red, two dogs yap as it passes the icy bench where two
    great babushkas sit, and it seems to carry off more time
    than a life will as it waits
A nail proves it
A portrait dangles from it
Our ink a pendulum
We'll work, I said
We walked
Scum fluttered in the mud
The sphinxes all utter glasnost
It is already endless
The unconscious sleeps in vain

Chapter Eighty-Five

The object of contemplation is between profiles
I remember being so
The walls multiply
The skies slide
O Gavronskaya
She longs for something whole, complete, entire, but when she
    encounters disintegration she greets it like her lover
She binds herself to observation
We wobbled in connotation
Ahead of us a woman was working a baby carriage on warped
    wheels through the gray-blue snow
In such a life is direction contemporary
As I did so
But one leg was slower than the other and she kept drifting to
    the left and then correcting herself
A colonel followed, the huge fingers of his gloves extended as
    stiff as pegs
Inadvertently a body is the direction of our existence

Chapter Eighty-Six

Our laborious luck is not submission
The cousin who was in prison was a crossed one
A great fish swallowed its father and swam up the Neva
One can have eggs for medicine, for covertness
But our response to the enormous risk was to rest in bed with
    surprising stubbornness
Our reposes are all alike, Vasya said
Buzz or pulse, Arkadii asked
But the officer's voice was so low the answering machine went
    off
When a thing resists me my back is numb
This represents a proclivity, a tilt
It extends to the thumb
A slight poisoning by nettles of whom it would be
Thoughts are exceptions enough
Discerned and sacrificed to the plans for expressing their
    results

Chapter Eighty-Seven

Here is a red kerchief, a good mother said to her son
Seven nannies, he answered, nurture a baby with no eyes
The colonel suddenly parked in a snowbank and set off from
    his truck at a run
Several hours went by, and he roared, as I descended
    congested rivers in my drunken truck
Zina, he shouted, it's your Papa come home — I have only one
    thing to say to your brothers: life is shit
History intoxicates the question "whom?" but not the question
    "who?"
So the colonel ran back over the twenty kilometers he had
    come
So the home in clouds leaves hills
A boy in the building had started playing a saxophone
Then his mother one night buried it in the garden under the
    vegetables
But the objects that we see in life will play their role
A cheap pirate album of Elvis songs called "Rock on the Bone"
The boy replaced the saxophone with stones
Trivialities or monstrosities — they are the same — the proof
    of one another

Chapter Eighty-Eight

I felt the proof of points but no continuum
But traditionally a novel integrates a person with the life it
    leads
We know a person slept because it slipped too far in snow
It identified in rice, in wine, in kitchen
It woke, but not where it had left off
And still I always read for awhile once I was lying on the sofa
Dream is duration with its grim expression
Duration desired behind the door
There is disintegrity in polarities as such
Every terminus spilling
It's like a nipple pulled — it halts
The exact moment of continuity in every corner
Experience nipped, doubled now in a short birch
But how can this be done, I asked

Chapter Eighty-Nine

Misha should be a major character in the Russian novel
Sasha, too, and Nadia
You will start with the third chapter, Arkadii said, and the first
   sentence must be attributed to Emmanuel Kant as follows:
   everything happens so often, that speaking of it makes no
   sense
You will meet people accompanying their ghosts, said Alyosha,
   and speak with them
Kolya, Shura, Borik, Sveta, Tanya, Natasha, Igor, Vladik, Vanya,
   and the other Misha
Zina stood on a chair
Arkadii waved the ghosts aside
There must be a sentence which claims a chapter for itself
And a name at the vanishing point in a person's description
So that the days will seem not to have gone by — and in fact
   names are relationships with a remarkable economy while
   descriptions are profligate
But pleasure is a mental process too as well as the producer of
   an aesthetic object
It is not what I knew
Our Russian workers like to dig holes, Arkadii said, while
   Americans prefer machines that scoop
The coincidence of experiences occurring with experiences
   already had produced identity — but it spills

Chapter Ninety

Subjects separate into themselves and then come out again
Four padded apertures round a sour air
The canals cannot tower
Subjects (that is, all of us — and we speak for ourselves) have
    the thirst of our finitude and we hoard unsatiated
    elaborations why
Without the conclusion of all these voluptuous stammerings a
    word is dead
Such which is as much as
But the unguiding present patience is without prepare
So enormous changeless caused and causeless events come
Cold lines of wind tightly weaving between hot lines of light
The neighbor, smoking on the landing near the communal
    slosh bucket, watching the descent of an aluminum pot
The damp ego climate, our picaresque obsequiousness
A man on the roof points toward a gap in the tower at the
    corner of the inactive church
Optical reality and uncertainty around
Alyosha lay his shirt over the chicken

Chapter Ninety-One

Metaphor hides the paranoia of writing
The speechless jogs of the horse
But metaphor may be scaled to the loves of life
Its increments associate with the practice of impressions
So the yardstick notes how the forest might be pocked
Agricultural workers buzzing the bronze and this less social
    than mystical
Of course the logger is indifferent to the suffering of his echo
Overhead the crows turned day and night
Rejection of closure, slapping of wings
Every night at the end of the sofa stood the kitchen
The metonym reduces the monument
A monument has the effect of jiggling and then forcing the
    lock
Beyond the door was a trampled pot
Graffiti of the horse in the corridor

Chapter Ninety-Two

The day awaits disaster
A growling crow is threatening to set fires
The old bathtub in the yard moans about its tired spine but
    cozies up to the filthy snow by casting its pink shadow
A collie has thrown itself into one of the canals
A woman carrying a bucket has slipped on the ice and is
    berating passersby for walking in her kvass
A crowd in trampled snow gathers at the trailer to trade old
    newspapers for coupons good for popular novels
Little Dima has secreted a message in the Monument to the
    Heroes of War saying that he is bored
A one-armed veteran from Afghanistan is wearing a black
    Mordred sweatshirt
Ostap has gone to an abandoned flat where the "Black and
    White" exhibition is installed to take a turn standing
    guard
No one is home — at this angle the white sky is reflected in the
    cup of blue tea
Without looking at a map, a person has made a real journey
The baggage is under America, which itself is red and brown
    and blue
These colors are improved on television
The night threatens perfection — a new chair has turned up to
    replace the broken one in the kitchen and Zina has found
    a chicken

Chapter Ninety-Three

One horde — and the man almost threw himself at it
Too much material and it halts
They simply do not gawk
Gawking slows crowds
In the vodka line the men were resilient — he sulked
I was drunk, said Vasya, and I'd staggered into the street to
    stop cars and announce that I wasn't their occupant
I am able to
Memory in repetition presents a self-sufficient object
All the prospects in themselves, and details ad infinitum
But each person must not seem to witness an episode with the
    most provisions
All fluttering subsides if it has goals
In these days people love and immure
We are never worried about the passage of time
We never forget

Chapter Ninety-Four

Well, how's the battle going, and who's the enemy
Four thugs came to the door and demanded
It is our right, said one wearing his medals
No one accepted responsibility for those medals
I remember the colonels' picnics, Arkadii said
The women spread the picnic blankets and attributed all the
    men's enthusiasm to the children so as to protect the
    dignity of the colonels
They blasted at the turtles
They undressed among the ants
Eventually the ink will run dry and the ants will die
And Pushkin's friends will describe everything to vegetables
They will do it in splendid epigrams: 1) the only competitor
    whom grass should fear is cucumber, 2) the expression "I
    understand" merely extends a vast tautology, 3) on the
    one hand it is difficult for me to believe that anything is
    actually here and on the other it is hard to accept that it is
    going away, 4) but at the same time a large proportion of
    human error comes from the arbitrary division of
    continuous motion into discontinuous elements
An epigram is for timing and typing
Those are strange luxuries in our society
Blameless recitations, lessons in music, the whole family went
    back for it

Chapter Ninety-Five

No teachers have gone to the village
No doctors were calling
We would have to wait long — the authorities are not
    obligated to regard anything as a romance nor officiate
    within a romantic perspective
The garlic lay on the windowsill
The sun stood on the canal
How do the Japanese gossip, I asked Malyavin
Vodonoy said it was consistent with agency
The official — like a grasshopper — scampered near the door
In America it is customary to catch an eye — some eye
There's a simple system of whose
Subtle — with twang, shackles, fold, street, waiting
The perpetual sex alternative, with complex repetition and
    simple combination
The women applauded — someone surrendered a chair
I see a body as a built thing, someone said

Chapter Ninety-Six

Her face is good
Her head is maybe too large, or it has too much cheek and too
    much neck
With aggressive and honorable tenderness she thought, this is
    no counterfeit necessity
There are microscopic hairs in the flesh
All sorts of intrigues
She felt relationship rather than existence
She passed it — the friend of a friend
We had American shampoo
They were in the bath and nude
Our flesh has no abundance
And can this be an American question
The work of a person
But no — her breasts are blind
Probably with the last light (pink and brown)

Chapter Ninety-Seven

Zina had opened a window and shaken the curtain down over it
Arkadii arrived at his chair
From nowhere Zina produced wine
Hunger reaches to pretend its meaning
A navy winter evening espionage
I have not seen one another since the war
The captain kept a straw in a drawer
His jeep was a launch, the sun a yellow tugboat, the lead drink
    a decent voice, an honest needle one that's threaded
I read a thousand letters and cut out the place names, the
    colonel said
I summoned the troops for an index
The cattle tracks mutter — in my land too — and burrs ride?
    collies?
Mother and Father — but Father has died, I replied — pulling
    my finger from hers
Is the time rubber?
One night I slept on amber

Chapter Ninety-Eight

If a man were a womanizer...
The man was a mumbler
Simply naming the people who die — but it's not interesting
I should touch his toes
I said to Vodonoy that my arm had been numb
You should touch your toes, he said, but you shouldn't
    succumb
We have before us time to return
Milky incandescent paths
An infatuation doesn't mean that life is bad
I should teach your toes
There was something really in the north — minus 50, Vladimir
    said
I was taken by dog sled to a women's prison
The strange place filled me at first with an envious and uneasy
    curiosity like that which people feel when they encounter
    a group of animals or some alien form of life that has no
    knowledge of them — but after a time, after I had been
    seated in front of the women to give my lecture, facing
    them as they sat in rows, after the guards (who were also
    all women) had moved to the back of the room behind
    them, here and there the prisoners began to . . .
Breasts and more than breasts

Chapter Ninety-Nine

As often as they walk they think
The genitals themselves are instruments of inspection
They faced the stage and their clothes opened and rose
They crossed
Fathomless shadows on the ground in the ice
The landscape was smudged, awaiting more snow
An undescribed immobilizing hour — one — I wanted to sleep
To sprawl — a woman clears her face
The advance is an almond
Who should teach almonds
Your almonds and mine
An eye is that piece of the brain shifted out and exposed
All well and when
Oval snows blew

Chapter One Hundred

Outside the mouth all is gray and green
But there's village and the dry violence there
Each morning one weakens and some moths issue like dogs
Thus the orange bus came pissing into the snow bank
The novel is without additional resemblance
And yet — things must put me in order

Song in Order

    Bed whose tongue was burned
    is turned by name excited
    Let's begin to everything
    To snow

    It's cold whose snow was turned —
    Recklessness makes difference
    But difference is slow and deaf
    to stone

    Life whose state was learned
    is made by name desired
    The city would state anything
    as home

    We slow to stone in name
    But we love without completion
    Life is complete at any turn
    to know

Rice and such erudition
Persons feed themselves in the small sense known
As I said to Arkadii, that one's your novel — you should call it
    War and Space
Each to protect an interest
A Pushkin
A bucket
Fine green sand
We are all incredibly lazy

Book Four

Chapter 101: A Day Long Awaited

Leningrad is a city of suspense
Life, death, time, and eternity — they are futurisms
We feel unrestrained in these relations
Meditatively ferocious we woke and watched the crows
They were displaying their emotions, they were not surrealist
Misha said, Russia is a nation of substitution and not of
    juxtaposition
So, does an American memorize and extemporize writings
The city was suspended
A few words
I would hear them uttered by someone six floors below
    between the dirty trees
Misha was breathing a tuneless but recognizable tune through
    his teeth
The coffee was complete in three froths
I can feel again the irritation of all saturation
Human as it is to saturate

Chapter 102: The Blue Man

A blue human of freezing rain stood awaiting the train
He was no continuation but a spasm
He then tried for a space to lay hold
An immediate answer had passed through his mind and he
    had accomplished durability of view
His eyes were the palest blue
A solitude of strain, collected, consumed
He was like a thwarted cocoon
Bits of this dark blue man contained alcohol
The weight of the man painting slogans
Such men are embarking accidents
Accidents condense — a fabulous tedium
Recollection without past, without basis
A blue brain, on terraces of matter
A burst of cold, a blinding corridor

Chapter 103: Internal Controls

Shores, borders, and letters
A story of safety
A storm that was cold to the point of comedy and no moon on
the laundry
I had asked about a shock of compromise
Hours by a picture to reconcile
We are afraid of continuity but not of conformity
A certain generalizing and even prophesying to be made
We make only an inferior acknowledgement but a choice
amounts to being called upon
Work — I could smell the books
Diesel, mint, hay
Dima told an anecdote — there's a certain prison in which the
inmates horde loose tea and they make of it a narcotic
syrup, but recently certain city workers have made
another, paralytic syrup, both syrups blue
I understand, I said — but it's poetics, not linguistics
The safety of delight, the sinking of coincidence
The weakness of nearly everyone who recognized each other
instantly

Chapter 104: An Anecdote is Perceived Through the Density of Observation

Gavronsky suffered from indifference, from a diminished
    sense of outrage
But Gavronskaya has set down the soup in buckets
The light suspended in the wet air loyally holds them
We don't worry, said Gavronsky, too much in a short time
Even though we don't rhyme — ever
We achieve fidelity, we engage in gluing, sucking, seizing, and
    fusing
Adherence is difference
We perceive and have another reason
Chronology is just another ratio
That is all merely painters' talk, said Gavronskaya, so now you
    will take some mother's talk
A preparation of domestic time — it is our defense against
    jealousy
The nationalist attacked but not for nation
He acted with an instinct for interference
He mistook himself for love

Chapter 105: Who Is Happy?

Description is racing perception against serenity
Yellow bracketing, pink realism
We walked through the hard yellow pockmarked door and left
    number 29 Nekrasova
We were in the steaming neighborhood on snow
The earth has a never-ending number
But no one has yet found fate (design)
There are increments of power but not of cup or bed
But there are estimates that apathy will manage
Let us think of anti-matter, the physicist had said — it must
    effect a sapphire
A sapphire is especially solid
He had lived on Nekrasova every night
Mineral vulnerability, Vitya said, is just fine feeling
Always the wind flies against the light
And the cigarette smoke is removed

Chapter 106: A Breeze on the Embankment

Every language is embanked, every speech sucked in
All our desires are synonymous
During all the outrages hung a note of some kind, and Olga's
    mother's sister was by the window singing
Olga was proud of the woman's heels — they were a vocal
    apparatus through the blockade
At night the blockade would burst into pieces
The people dined on belt
We had eyes of rust and blue
We reflected our sky, the old woman said
Torches snapped in our fingers
No day without seduction and every seduction was timed and
    amplified
We had a great stubborn clock in the head — it was like the
    gossip of a hammer
But now, she said, habit and history, they seem the same
Life has no end, and they are complete
And I compare them very patiently

Chapter 107: Winter Again Called In or Out

The moon was not thinking but the imprint of a hand was on
    its face
Then eclipsed by a single simple thumb
Proportions of near and there
Proportions which are flat but should be round
Then did you fear the KGB? I asked
They were very ridiculous and then they became polite
And who do they call by both name and patronymic — they
    are now each other, face to face
The ice was whining and singing in thaw
An incident resounded for the fifth time
Insistent
Assistance
None of that was meant
The neighbors' windows tapped by dripping glass faced across
    the way
Layer by layer warm onions surrendered

Chapter 108: An Achievement

We were so rested by winter that now only the hand can spread
The palpable linings of objects and reverse crevices are turned
A whole plot was inhaled and no cough came of it
Continual states, independent states, and contiguous states of
      consciousness
One night we were talking with Dima while Nastia simpered
      with the deepening requirements of fortunes of
      consciousness
Spring and a deepening of spring
Responsibilities are incurred
And instead a sense of invisibility and relaxation
Every month has a sleep hammering at something right
      against the head
Each alteration produces communication and disproves the
      little rural paths running through the wilted birches
      between housing blocks
Certain texts, said Dima, are characterized not only by an
      aesthetic but also by a scientific function — these cause an
      attentive reader to become conscious in a practical state
A little yellow car was circumventing the path
So much to circumvent in memory
Even clumsily we have relaxed, Dima said

Chapter 109: A Change of Season

And so in a truly magical manner it has come about in
    apparently one continuous morning that I have become
    the possessor of multitudes of wide open windows and of
    sunlight tumbling into other minute fissures of an almost
    invisible brightness — why not see in this a special
    meaning?
Matter, substance, has become so weightless that it can't
    absorb damp or accumulate moisture, so the wind carries
    it soundlessly past the pale jade scales that float between
    the branches of the blossoming pine trees and against the
    outstretched water in the Neva which however feels
    nothing, reflects nothing
Four days of warm weather have passed
Can it really be four?
And for me, in defiance of the laws governing the despondent
    progression and movement and alternation of days, no
    end has broken or bound off the hour in which I returned
    home and stretched a white cloth over the balcony like a
    tent which has been flapping in the wind ever since, for
    signs of heat and soon the first tints of humidity will
    appear, though the unbearably white sun now hangs
    immobilized in a strontium-turquoise dusty sky declining
    imperceptibly towards some boundary which is too
    speculative to allow one to differentiate anything from
    anything else, day from night — and night itself now, in
    any case, is like a candle burning in the morning — and
    should some 10 p.m. arrive it will fill the room at last with
    the first rays of humidity, their saffron-yellow seething
    against my pitiful tent, which offers no protection, now
    abruptly sobbing when the wind suddenly changes

direction, until all at once it is blown away and falls into the branches of the trees below the balcony

This reminds me of the juggler who was discovered in a church juggling fruits because he had no other "language"

A sense of insane optical clarity at all levels alternated with the flashing heat of his hands moving in a predatory measured pace toward some materialization that is like language, despite the intense feeling of uncertainty that touches these objects, until they are no longer even necessary

Into that marvelous breach of silence, into the instantaneously growing abyss at the point of "maximum stress," gushed something he called happiness

On the evening of the first day I had a splitting headache

I spent the whole night on the balcony anticipating no end to morning or night and no end to my headache which had turned smooth and straight, like a path leading to some condition which is difficult to explain but which has nothing in common with time

The next day I took the metro and then a bus to some nearby lakes, where I stumbled onto an abandoned tennis court behind clusters of wood-lilac yellowing amid fiery blue-grey pine needles

However there is a danger that life, being narrated, will turn into an "adventure," and every adventure moves inexorably towards resolution — but how can I say that I don't like adventure?

I think now of the truly startling antiquity of the sensation that *this is happening*

Chapter 110: Repairs to the Painter's Studio

The hues and saturation of the heat and the prisms of the cold
    can hardly be compared — they are — to a compulsive
    consciousness
Gavronsky's studio was to be seized but old
Gavronskaya was hunting
I've begun to stalk, she said one night, a very clever girl on
    Pestelya
Particulars are always true
Gavronsky views
Everyone recognizes the table or the corner or the window,
    but it's really no table, not even a real room, he said
The girl is like an abbess in rooms in abeyance — they are
    awaiting a hotel there and she attends
Here's an occupation, Gavronskaya said to her
A painting needs more explanation than a small gold bracelet
It was yellow at noon between a green wall and a pink one
A whole day is not an entity — no sun standing on linoleum
It is like nothing without restlessness
Without regular brushes
Without exaggeration

Chapter 111: Away from the Center of the Scene

I caught the new phrase flowing out in a whisper
Sex will begin again
A bench began
What talk we took in hand
But one doesn't care what to do in a rain
One can say that sex has featureless density
It's true
But it's true too — sex is all feature and has no destiny
An enormous toe, a dusty skin, breast hair
Eyes open at the edges — we have eyes between our legs
Nothing is unblinking
Where else is your face
At such an age the features fatten
Our mouths are not moths any more and our eyes are not ants

Chapter 112: Counting from One

The Astonished Clock bristled with yellow in the trees
Seasons are obscene, said some man on the path coming
    home in a spattered coat
He added bridges
It's the man with the dancing collie, Zina whispered
My god, said Arkadii, and I can't forget how the girl in the
    hard currency shop smiled
It's *glasnost*!
It crowds our pages
It's a bell off to the left
Appalling trees to kiss
But what will put us in our coffin
Gavronsky had put the coffin in a corner
It's part of a sequence, he explained — it's lethargically
    continuing to be
Zina made a little jump on the ice in the way and skated
    forward in her boots
I made for the side with a handful of leaves

Chapter 113: The Baffled Corner and the Saigon Cafe

I put on my glove and took up a coffee
It is best
Groups of people mostly strangers averted similarly
It is very notorious
A supervisor under its chin appeared with a wet gray rag
Granny to granny I'll tell you, she said, you know what's alive
    when it gets to its feet
Abbreviation
Abbreviation
You see how little my feet are
Boots made of crows through the windows
On the wall my father had a puppet horse, Natasha said
Truck value — complete value — invaluable value
Invisibility had reached its limits
My window is its own well-being, Arkadii said

Chapter 114: Late At Mitya's with the Swedish Attache

The Swedish attache had two parts
He was called Maximus
So speaking of himself, he said to Olya
Then a second silence fell on the room
The angel of silence hovered over
We need more wine, Natasha said
Maximus! — we will go West
The night hardly exists here — it's a mere smoke
A plate of bread with salt fish stood on the bed
They are Prebaltic lyrics, Mitya said, against misfortune and
    justice
Kolya was singing in the second room

> *We cannot help but here be sober*
> *Life on earth is almost over*
> *Red lips, red lips, always open*
> *Over, over, often over*

It is a boogie, Kolya said — I call it the boogie of my rest
The boogie of night
That is a weakness which I am filling — with seagulls in my tea

Chapter 115: Squeaking Planks Over the Mud

We've green and yellow mud, said the man in the spattered
coat
The spring has turned so cold even the muck is reflecting the
sky
Why can't science balance the temperature?
I've got nerves of steel, said the old granny to him — she was
attempting to drag her dog back toward her but the long
rope had gone twice around a tree
But what's in your pocket?
Maybe I'll save it yet!
The other granny laughed — Andrei Vasilievich, I knew you
before my life
Well somebody saved your life, Natalia Borisovna, and it wasn't
me
A taxi came around the far building, heaved at a pothole, then
turned onto the footpath and continued the man
Are you fishing for compliments, Andrei Vasilievich, here on
the banks of our swamp?
Hah, he said, I'd only catch crocodiles
The big dog had made another turn around the tree
Listen to this mud — all it does is squeak

Chapter 116: Aesthetic Gratification

Arkadii, I said
What in your opinion is the quintessential Russian novel?
The Life of Arseniev
But we can't decide anything
A word runs across a page and the page is torn
The sun is just a balanced coin
Sincerity is secondary to expressiveness
Rusty light collects on the taxis
Pollen fills the holes in the old spider web
Reality is copied — we do it with our eyes
Things have complete impunity in my thoughts
My idea of the neighbor is harmonious smoke
My mouth emits smoke
We did not fulfill our obligations

Chapter 117: The Destinies of Observation

A Russian novel should be called *The Adherent*
It is obsequious
It holds
It is opportune
I'm an observer of another kind, maybe a blind kind, Ilya said,
    but completely faithless
If I am a postcontinualist, said Arkadii, logic dictates that I be
    the only one
So my granny was a great precontinualist
My grandmother could perform an amazing feat with an egg, I
    said
An egg, a broom, and a glass of water
In an anti-cliche (like an earthquake) to make one sentimental
Provoking healthy excitements the egg thuds
An inert theme — searching, buying, and serving
Everything depends on actuality, Zina said
With such a phrase one can imagine another world

Chapter 118: On Postcontinualism

Here's the same humming shake of the roof, the milky sun,
     threads of shadow
The weather is syntax
Thus we can speak of a cold of poetry
But I want confirmation
Something more Western than jeans
It is completely impossible to say I want a job
What does someone mean with such an expression?
Horses and dogs
Sunlight simultaneously from ten points of the compass
Inevitably you cultivate within yourself something like
     blindness
Be calm, you say, but I notice it's said with a certain flexibility
Tranquillity changes toward morning into a thick sapphire
     drop
With "poetical longing" I want to transcribe thevoice of the
     refrigerator: mmmmmmmmmmmmmmm
Thus the phenomenon of refrigeration becomes
     comprehensible

Chapter 119: A Problem Posed by Interpreting Dreams

What problem was my mind attempting to solve with a dream
    of two pigeons injured by a cat
Philosophy depends on our having perceived a difference
    between empty and full
They occur in different fields of time
They provide different satisfactions
So, Alyosha said, we have an avant garde of the expanded word
    and an avant garde of the compressed word
Let me explain —
But we were interrupted
Milovsky had removed his shoes and come in
His presence was so quiet that conversation stopped
Arkadii and Alyosha went to a corner to smoke
The idea of *in Russia* was dispersed into rain
It was not a world view but an empty moment
Different immigrations, Natasha said — I believe we have
    witnessed an enchanted immigration and now we see an
    immigration that's completely — one could even say
    perfectly — disenchanted
Alleys, owls, pillows, riddles

Chapter 120: One Spring Morning

Divination by clouds must be renounced under a colorless sky
Ostap produced a small cardboard device for divining mood
A staircase
The proportions of temperaments and moods
Zina ran a rag over the table
I turned on the gas for tea
It's a blind day, Zina said
Such a sky produces vast absent-mindedness
Here
Arkadii and then I produced gloom
I too, she said
The device had turned a foreboding greenish black
Papa, it's just a human revelation, said Ostap — such colors
       grow from temperatures and salt
You see? — heliotrope means passion

Chapter 121: Zina Calls Me Her Sister

We sat in the common abstraction
Hulls of two halves of a Cuban grapefruit lay on one white
    plate
What does it mean?
Changing rice
Attachments are very distant
We were planning the information
It's maternal — and not carried further
A search
We are at an advantage
We are very relaxed with sophistication
Lifting dishes
The future — we agreed absolutely
And how could one wish back toward something in the past
Do you feel that you're feeling time?

Chapter 122: We Meet Rosa and Mitya in the Vyborg
While Nationalists Clamor in the Center

Modernism recognized things, postmodernism disperses them
But I can't think wishfully
I have no sense of direction, that particular form of
    self-consciousness
Every kind of internal speech is continuous
But this nationalist speech — it's external, Mitya said
One absolutely must have a sense of direction if one's to hate
    the West
And with what sense does one hate the Jews?
It's a purely rhetorical question
The world was created in a void — it's the manifestation of
    non-existence and creation was a non-event
In this case the wind is perennially rebuilding tradition and
    tradition consists of chaos and intensification
The weight of a place displacing the weight of its time is
    nationalist
Postmodernist displacement puts things in places
And what have we truly experienced
The intensity, said Rosa, of empty places

Chapter 123: The Three-Day Silence of the Telephone

At this point my life can be neither too short nor too long, said
    Lydia Yakovlevna, leaning heavily on the table
So what reality, what logic is improved when they replace a set
    of one-digit numbers with another of the same length
From where he was sitting Kolya reached the pot on the stove
    and added water to the tea
They are doing it district by district, Alyona said
Outside it wasn't yet dark and past the kitchen window blue
    rain mixed with yellow snow was falling
It's an old district, said Lydia, and now we have silent
    telephones — a traditional sentimental motif but here in
    fact it's part of real experience
Sometimes in situations like these thousands of worlds are
    speaking to themselves
From habit
But habit is a dynamic only in everyday time
The further away the more aestheticized habits become
Bloated arms, open palms
That silence breaks the connections between me and this
    world, Lydia said
But speech doesn't guarantee an object
It is the image of personality not the mechanism that sets it in
    motion that's important

Chapter 124: The Pity That It's So Good

Balancing like a piece of paper the window rattled in the wind
A familiar rocking tugboat stood on pockets of the hive
Arkadii's bare feet rested on the radiator
There's no melody in peacefulness — it sinks in the smelly
     lapping waters of deafness
It's a pity we're only half-deaf, I said
Music is an exaggeration, he answered, but I was distracted
My disintegrating personality was completely relaxed
It's as pragmatic as the weather, the wind and the watery
     figures it makes with its fingers in the rain
Voluptuously it makes a blot on the page, then sketches onto it
     wings and a beak and releases this bird of irresponsibility
     to float off into the world
You Americans want to confess everything, Arkadii said
But the weather was unimposed
Though watching it idly sustained a moment of anguish
A swooning of the heart over connotation
It's strange to what extent we sometimes try to defend our
     work

Chapter 125: Everything in Life is Significant

Flattery?
We even ask lyrical questions of ourselves
Clanging?
The sound includes all of our contemporaries
Responses hasten
We must constantly care for our conversational health!
Black eyes, blue skin
Responses halt
It's your turn to speak again
The earth fruits and the trees vegetable
Our tasks shift our panegyrics
Such is our willful life
And it's so simply erotic
Who else but the man through the branches would be our
    neighbor?

Chapter 126: The Doubting Man

We had found a pretext for not going out — swarms of such
    pretexts are here every day to engulf us
Ellipses
Memories
These and similar outcries
The gloomy daylight was condensing like steam on the
    windows
Outside, below, in the patch of forest confined to the housing
    block a tattered cat howled as the cold tugged its fur
Nobody — Arkadii laughs as he coughs
Coffee is a savage consolation for waking up
And tea?
The same, but like a sun
Its savagery is only metaphysical
The strictness of the walls of the room had been lost —
    withdrawn or removed
Here, said Arkadii — a letter from Chekhov
One must always suspect the beginning and end, since it's
    there that the writer puts his lies

Chapter 127: A Vulnerable Apparatus

I had read a law as a child where it was posted —
    expectoration forbidden
The scratching of my name
Such spitters were addressed by those words on the wall
The clarity creeps
Fish? Arkadii asked
Out on the street in the sun Vitya was borrowing another
    man's passport so that we could buy cheese
Zina had gone down into a shop across the street
No distance, no form
The humidity was rising in chapters
No time, no verse
Lack of sleep and unequal recollections of the pleasure
    regulate the rosy non-narrative
Everything is normal — this is to be underscored
The spitter tried
This is conscious

Chapter 128: Are Banalities Necessary?

You may say the sentence, Mayakovsky is a man of the people,
    but you cannot free it
Perfection
It has every direction
Dostoevsky too is a man of the people
Aretha Franklin is a man of the people
Some people are moved to know every detail of a specialty
Possessed of a special kind
A different man speaks of a cosmopolitan man
Maybe Lenin, maybe nations
Buildings
Lips
The warm toppling drifts of poplar tufts
We do not have a poetry that would combine words like
    bibliophile sugars
But we know such humid shifts

Chapter 129: A Mother's Worry

At the door of the room Gavronskaya fussed
For you to go to the West?
With her wild bitterness the mother loved maudlin pictures
She imagined herself in the part of the younger sister in a
    romance involving a landscape painter
She means nothing, said Gavronsky
There are four and should be two
It is neither more nor less than a mother's love and the
    irritability of its object
The object's preparation
The landscape's vindication
The unchanging scene with its thick muddy field and furrows
    of high sketchy grass on either side of the empty road
    rising from right to left in summer depicts the protest of
    the young
What kind of separation lies in wait? Gavronskaya asked
A rooster's promises, quoted Gavronsky
Katya came in with more toast and melted cheese
Mothers too leave their families, said Gavronskaya

Chapter 130: Who Reads Dostoevsky?

Hills, walls — calm and stained
Despite the shadows of the leaves on the window there wasn't a
    spot on the floor
Fifty birches were rising and falling
An adolescent, reading, doesn't look around even once — is it
    some tension of age that prevents me from expending all
    my attention?
And what is it I want now from a book?
With curiosity I watched a head moving through the grass
The sentences could not be divided
Outside they say, let well enough alone
Inside they say, don't step outside
Here's an extreme situation
My figure would disappear
It is harder to breathe then — the number of sentences
    doubles, triples
I determine to penetrate this strange process of humble poetic
    longing
Love? will?

Chapter 131: The Brevity of Limbo

The baby was bound on the balcony as the sun set
Any other available baby is defective later than its mother
And shame is followed by a miraculous recovery
It's as if any child emerged from gold sky
Below, the surface of the Neva wriggled with the continuity of
     a tree
An insert pressed against her belly — to give a look of
     pregnancy
I thought I'd been achieved and then undivided
Below in the winter light stood the white buildings
Three grannies in wool coats stood in the frost watching their
     granddaughters conspiring in fur bonnets
Our history is not limbo but a wide erasure, said the official
For example, my son has joined a rock band called the Free
     Masons and they dance naked and play saxophones
The angel of forgetfulness has many feathers, said a granny
It brings the heat of summer
And it resembles waiting

Chapter 132: Something Perceived With Peripheral Vision

We paused on the Palace Embankment
There are always monstrous prepositions, colors, murky
    juxtapositions, and flux more vast than distractions, more
    lasting than the past, in the Neva
Ducks float by
Two sullen men in blue fish
I wonder why their plurals are the same as their possessives
It's the famous Leningrad wind, Arkadii said
The words *bomb, drawer, towel* — they tumble over night, under
    your arm, between your cheeks
Diverging eternities — they resemble suspicions
But the reality surrounding us is not immediately forced into
    art
Nostalgia is just sprung compassion
By the way, it's never too cold for the grannies
Their life now is inordinately colloquial, because they have to
    go somewhere
What about that old woman arguing with herself in the
    kitchen? I asked
In such a case everyone else goes somewhere

Chapter 133: A Living Space Bursting with Delight

Lyosha, I said, please
Explain to me the two avant garde traditions after Mandelstam
    and Pasternak
With no indolence, he said
But, for example — can one say that a huge sun is a damp
    whole in English
It would be very difficult, I said
For instance, I could not have said so before 1985
Unbirth and birth
No, prebirth
Nonbirth
Petersburg
I agree
Let me put it this way: where is the moment of the greatest
    consolidation, the greatest potential, the moment just
    preceding a burst of color, the moment guaranteeing the
    greatest density of color
This has something absolutely to do with courage
It was material sliding, silent, strange, quiet

Chapter 134: The Force of Conditions

A fish swam outside the human half-skull
I really don't know how, I said, to use that petty authority
Such is your irony — seen at a distance
Silence
Not thing but volume — it's true of me
There are only mobile states of mind, accepted provisionally as
    one's own
Wet snow, convictions
There is no distribution to sustain, just an egg within an egg
Intense, voluntary patience
It's force, not form
Woolen odors
And events which are irrevocable, not to be thought of
But I fear them as much as lost opportunities
It's as if spite were the opposite of fate

Chapter 135: The Formative Properties of Words

I cannot imagine a glass prose
But I was losing interest in the phenomenology of my dreams
Daylight was thicker than it seemed — with augmentation,
    odor, air
Where are words changed?
Kuzmin, for example, had challenged the potential bliss of
    transcendence with the beauty of the world
And I trust this lust
I can't know what I've missed
Shallow dreams fall, follow
They appeal to words
It's the principle of connection not that of causality which
    saves us from a bad infinity
The word *hunt* is not the shadow of an accident
That hunger had no exotic antecedent
It's an ordinary shifting in a line forming near a shallow
    stairwell
That's where I waited

Chapter 136: A Bad Cough

I sat on the big couch — the rain on the window had increased
     the yellow size of what was outside — where I was feverish
America is a great cure, Arkadii said
In my opinion . . . no . . . well, of course it's natural to look
     back longingly at the brink of experience
A great curve
Everyone hurries to sit on it
Dark arched branches were smudged against the housing
     block
So — we can imagine that Pushkin massaged the trunk of the
     tree there
A birch, its brain in white
The glass bent around the onion
And some translucence around that
Rain fell, but even the irregularity of the drips couldn't
     obliterate the rhythm that attaches occasion to memory
The telephone rang — America drifts
It scarcely disturbed
The senses had risen to greet another freedom

Chapter 137: Promise of a Summer Day Someday in the Crimea

A flat black rock will gleam, swallowing the light out of the sea
Hairy silk and the smell of salt crossing my hand
As twilight falls, the clams are pounded over coals
Declivities in the rock, abandoned by nature, occupied by man
And woman, I said
But of course, said Lyosha
In the distance only height and depth, a minimal sky
We will analyze the conventional language of socks and shirts
        and cheese and edges and clocks
A wall of freedom
A shore
People have mistaken yearning for enthusiasm
That's flirtation
Procrastination
It's fish in the dark — and we laughed at the pronunciation

Chapter 138: It's Impossible to Eat a Chicken Shot With a Stick

A man in a dark coat twisted a button in increasing light
And I speak, aim, with precision
In his patriotism the colonel had digressed and become inert
Now a woman with a feather in her hat was crossing a sunken
    path
The scene had a somber power
I'd be stung by music and on an appendage
But I'd misjudge hunger — it puts words in the mouth
The restoration of metaphysics is achieved with a variant of
    pointedness
Ilya stuck — and he had not been tentative about the death of
    the object at the strange yellow table covered by cakes
Tania posed for a snapshot holding open a cookbook with
    Stalin's introduction
"It is precisely this that solves the dilemma of existence
    established in the light of the Russian kitchen"
We were sitting in a reflected room
Sometimes my body does things and I just don't notice, Vanya
    said
A certain side, with certain symptoms, of consciousness

Chapter 139: Drama But No Outcome

A dog with its throat cut lay at the edge of the forest
We should collaborate on such suspicious cliches — they're
    formed every day — and make interpolations
Waiting depends on the thickness of thought
Its destiny — everything turns fortuitous
The plot stops, then description clocks thought
We wait from it
Waiting not waiting but sky
Everything is perpetuated
A woman with a tremor was watching us
She has recognized your celebrated foreignness, Arkadii said
Your past
No one wanted to be photographed
No one wanted to be kept in sight
Something would come to an end then

Chapter 140: A Sex and Shield

The phrase *passive verb* came to me in a constant
A sudden chill will seem to me
A vertigo
The hands really are so often cold but the fingers turn at the
     back
There was that sex of response that turned back responsibility
And a habit with no proof of its truthfulness
The mind is sent to the blood and blanks — in my experience
By whom I was seen, on what bench I was seated but a bench
     alone, from which the snow had been brushed away
The scene was utterly colorless and my attention was devoured
     by it as if it were dark
One hundred feet away a line swelled then thinned again and
     swayed
Its particular strength (its delayed volition) was suddenly
     toppling me
This is an immobile scene, without representation, Arkadii said
     abruptly, turning up fifteen minutes early in the park
     outside the building where he had gone to meet a certain
     Grisha
I was seeing the colors from the back
The horizons at the disposal of the colors

Chapter 141: The Genders of Everyday Life

We have split for many occasions
Arkadii!
Ho!
I disagree with you, I said
And I agree, he said — you're right!
About postmodernism
A city of genres
Take a naked doll and spoon, a lifted city
A great pastiche
You're wrong
I was straightening the blanket around where I sat, while Vasya
    turned up the tape machine
An unfinished conspiracy
Love and they are odd — a mounting context
We love the sexes of conditions we never leave

Chapter 142: The Explanation of the Dancing Tea

Flakes of falling sand slid over flash cards onto the slush in the
    path where we were walking from the bus stop to the
    housing block and I stopped to see what they said
Strawberry and wet — wet as dogs in tea
And heavy as luggage described as full of books
Do you read poetry
Limbs larger than cold, links lifted from the tang of the body
Strong, bare, and objective — these and other invalid
    categories are like a cat on a bed
Aleksei, I said, when I was slipping off my boots — your cat is
    bigger than your dog
Well — perhaps so
There is a book published in English said to be written by
    Shostakovich in the style of Zoshchenko, I said — do you
    read translations
I'd said such sex in detail, timing that spot of time
Our authenticities are often of detailed concern
The flow of speech is often dispersed in separate words
And I was summarizing my surprise
Here, said Paulina — the water's very good for tea

Chapter 143: The Onion Metaphor

Comparisons are frequent in language situations
Chances chosen after extra searches
Several layers out a yellow glint is a clinging purple button
Replacements don't surpass loyalty
The sea black as oyster
The speed of ant legs on water
I can't name where I don't know I sit
Happenstance closed and we were in it
At the theater doors a certain bulk of person guarded
The onion is absolute, said Vitya
The golden baldness holds no different brain
Art should be about decisions, Vanya said — or else choices
    are just chances that you steal and spoon
A regimen is not a system
Nothing was never was

Chapter 144: Description

My description gives my face in space, my story changes it
All narration is set with change
Atheism now is an adequate description, as free as air, as
    independent as fire
But in an era without religion, you can't tell an infidel from a
    buffalo
Maybe my face was set with fate
But my narration was embraced by particular rubble
Some broken concrete, a length of pipe, a poster proclaiming
    memory defaced
The grannies gathered close to see the excitement
They stared at my coat
You have gone to the incredible lengths of material prosperity
    and far from having disappeared you have turned up
    awaiting the 100th bus
But what's funny will turn out sad if you stand in front of it
    long enough
So it's essential to know how to sleep and at what time
The grime's scraping on reason reflected the face
    self-consciously
They waited and the drama sank in later

Chapter 145: A Digression That Differs from Description

The context to the incident almost killing Gavronsky had
    come out
The nationalist was a certain Nikolai not unknown to Katya
There'd been some history — so why not a nightmare from
    this Nikolai
Kolya's knife, Sasha's line
Katya is one of many flowers in our town, Rosa said, and they
    all make their usual Soviet smell
It was Gavronskaya she waited to tell
Sasha Gavronsky glowered
Speak in English, he said, so I don't understand your gossip
Well, it was your mother and Katya who solved the crime
Sasha shrugged
Quails like to snuffle in the woods — so they set out the bread
    and went there
Sasha remained
Suddenly having understood, I felt at last acknowledged
Certain changes had been delayed

Chapter 146: Whose Comedy Was That

Is real life prophetic if its details are typical
The unconstructed life cannot have been invented
Whose tragedy is that whose narrating "I" attaches itself here
     and there to the matters of my own fate
Such a pantheist making mind
I embrace that particular rubble
Embracing free willism despite the constant change of detail
Yellow shadow of the white facade of a poultry shop one day,
     green shadow the next
Arkadii pulled off a dirty sock and used my scissors to snip at
     his toe nails
He held up a snippet with pathos
Where is a chicken
Held up to a sequence of days interspersed by nights my
     snippet is sad
I desire disorder
Or order, the invention of desire
What would tell the narrator who I am

Chapter 147: Poetry is a Genre of Constructed Life

A true agent of culture must have a generous nature
All human, with human action
A granny or grandfather from irreducible shock
The world improves the word
That is, its admissibility
And the followed world
My life must be the form of my person who lives it and likes it
    cold and wet
A light holds my overcast humidities to the round
A tempo
A tendency
So form is the time
And desire is still dormant in a preliminary moment prior to
    belief in it
Self-consciousness eludes me
Self-consciousness gets ahead with the force of my
    independence (not bounded by self) and invention

Chapter 148: Impositions

I found myself on the sofa and caught a mineral water bottle
The face blowing steam with lips rolled
The blotches were blanketed
I saw the turtle's head emerge, only in the opposite direction
We were tangled without special need, after a continual lack of
    redundancy
Of tendency
Here's an instant of time continually endured
Death is its string
We were secured — but my breast was stretched into forms of
    face
I changed positions of face
The face going under hair and usually facing right
The silent face wanting me to describe it
I can't address the future, I'd feel too foolish
There is no act only state that's mirror

Chapter 149: The Poem under Number

We met Vitya on Gorkova counting against a bulge of stone
Twenty years ago, just here, I encountered a great
    mathematician
He asked me to guess what poem was buried between the
    sheets of numbers in his bag
And I guessed immediately what poem lay there
What kind of separation waits
Quoting was something everyone needed
It was in time and under number
It was a ceaseless consequence
My increments, I said, are hard to memorize
Once in Moscow I was asked to recite and the man was
    antagonized
Even "it" is irregular
There are irregularities for all that's permitted
Or I see it backward
Or it has its choice of contemporary resemblance

Chapter 150: The Sphere On the Embankment

The exact novel genre — satirical or resonant
There is maybe too much non-literary evidence for it
But irritations without controversy are an inspiration for
    authority
We were leaning on the balustrade beside a chipped rock
    sphere
Zina will find slippers and we will wait
Patience is the inspiration for influence
We blanked at broken gliding ice and pink stripes on the water
Nothing but always
It's in passage
A ball in warning
Literary rolling
A woman on a bicycle with warped wheels
A woman with a birch broom
I didn't change it

Book Five

Chapter 151

Someone watches
Heavy marvels
So many arms of Marx
And marches
There is no match
Just coincidence
And that affinity which catches
Contrast — contrast is protracted
Someone hopes in marvelous withering
The marble muds of winter fracture
Elegy is their defender
And metal jealousy
A blue hue's action
A mental penalty and bastion

Chapter 152

The cold low, the white in a light, the yellow in sight
It is the amazing enormous apparatus
It is fascinating to be afraid and not to possess it
Details of tender response to a violence not seen
I mean I have my experience but do I give it
It requires a high level of consciousness along with loss of self
The authority of waking is lost
I sympathize by talking and taking in sleep
I cannot synchronize waking scale — if a person lives self-
    consciously it must be in a distant land — but the clock of
    observation sits on the kitchen table
And that is the scarab, Arkadii says, pointing at the small green
    TV
It is scale and ballad
And a painting is an eye-socket — or, no, a novel is
I've never dreamed of Leningrad, I said
I can't because it has no screen

I have mentality but no community in sleep
Just solitude and furnishings — film in seconds ending
Silly cossacks on tummies roll
After silliness there is nothing
Words, sentences
Modern muds don't take those things
So one day I asked, "Zina! Arkadii!"
Arkadii said he slept
But insomnia returns to body, Zina said
In claustrophobia our insomnia woke us
Softly awakened unjust blame
A woman is hunting for sleep, but she is sleeping to hunt
Contrast is not macho
Contrast is the crow in light

Chapter 154

The tint in the weather and yet another tint
They are exhaustive
Hints
But the hunt is intelligible
There is stagnant humidity and ozone
Animosity and lack of remorse that provoke at the same time a
    love intrigue
Perhaps we are reaching the end of the era of the three great
    determinisms
The end of the eros of a terminus
Here the poetic method requires an exercise of free will
Love provokes the exercise of frost
But we can't keep on always curled in the same way
We must curl in reverse
We must curl in cruelty
We must eat

Chapter 155

The spirit is residual and nothing martial
The air smelled of dust — of humidity, ash, and snow in the
    pollen
Of cold and crows
I prepared without clothes
A tiny hard apple held dull and dry in the hand
Languages
A code of sleep
As I dreamed I forgot, and woke pressed
Sleep is much the same thing
Even now I remember the bed
The wool was wet
The air smelled of garlic and coffee
The neighbor slept
Sleep is an intense contentment — its conditions are mine, its
    conditions are met

Chapter 156

I blinked in the pink of the grit
"Nyet!"— the shopkeeper's answer provided
Footstamping and athleticism — we are bullies
Nyet
The hunt in its orient bulging
It is hunting tinted
But everything is shaped — and nothing misshapen
There's disorder, humidity — but where there's nothing
    there's no termination
The moon in the mist hunts a chicken
The shop had only a cat, rice, and sparrows, but the sparrows
    had shat on the rice
So the product didn't coincide
The crowd riding tints surged out nonetheless all for apples —
    but at home we had apples
We are all deceived as selfish
The shop was ineffable and green

Chapter 157

We can take no time, we can take no light, but they appear and
    we have accounts
New pictures and defects
No objects
The poetic — this means loaned
Daily life presents matters for practical reason (free will)
Or it isn't so
There are parts of the light — agency, green, pink, and grime
No subject to light, and no discontent with life
Zina shrugged when I wanted to speculate
No innate love of forms
Then dispersal and reform
And Misha? — we laughed
It is impossible to study it all equally
Our curiosity cannot be practically applied

Chapter 158

Great calm is an objection
A deep frost rises and then sleep proceeds
An enormous sleep composed
A vast subordination
In the solitude of thickness, weight — on an ice — each night I
    was a fossil
But I was not witness
Or sometimes my sleep was reduced to its kitchen
The steams were trapped
I dreamed of hunters
One night I dreamed of the concentration that is haunted
Each hand seen, and the objects of momentum thicken
Russian
With caution
Suddenly I realize that my dreams sustain no skepticism

A young and beautiful woman who was repugnantly
　　supercilious and perfectly cold in the close dark cafe with
　　only two tables, six chairs, and a ledge along the wall was
　　eating ice cream in small pretentious increments with a
　　broken spoon, her feet resting on shards of broken glass
　　on the floor, which, when she rose, she maliciously kicked
　　in the way of customers entering the cafe in steaming
　　coats, blind from the white light on the snow outside
She had made a sentimental beginning — it was very boring to
　　me
Her general acceptance of schemata and cliches
The woman needs to balance
The woman needs to believe
But she was cruel
And my description then was an introspection of the system
We know something
We scarcely self-create
The self is long interested in the psychology of creativity
　　because it is a part of "living life in general"
At that moment a mud-splashed bundled granny pushed
　　through the door with two naked chickens hanging in
　　each hand by their dead yellow legs
You stupid old granny, someone yelled, don't wag your
　　business around in here
My business is finished, she answered
You can wipe your window with your ass

Chapter 160

There is any leaning listener in this Leningrad
It goes with no introduction
It was no one — or only someone
There are only interims to be seen — interims and particles
And is it something Russian between
None of our famous writers were Russians, Vasilii said
Pushkin?
African
Many divided continuations characterize the work
And Gogol's phobia?
Exacted
Actuality begged if Gogol couldn't greet
He was terrified that he'd be buried alive
There is evidence that he alone was justified

Chapter 161

Abash, abashed
One left reality
It was evening off the Neva at Vasya's and we were eating
    honey and drinking spirits from his grandmother
There's a man from my village, Vasya said, who is from a
    Christian sect not believing in killing
It was talk of Siberia
And Vasya's grandmother for thirty years had refused to say
    even a word there
A skidding of happiness and different inhibitions
Border war or civil war
Soldiers in the Afghan war
This subordination of one experience to two grammars is
    impossible in non-literary systems, Vitya said
This man was falling at the front from behind
He was thinking obsessively for support of a striped crosswalk,
    of salt fish and pickles, of tea the color of the sky, of snow
    and smoke on his grandmother's roof
Seryozha was dancing beneath his hollow face
Alyessa stood on the table and proclaimed that Seryozha
    couldn't kiss

Chapter 162

For how long couldn't Seryozha kiss
It was only during the degeneration of his versatility
Versatility must be habitual
Versatility must not become contortion
Our value, your value — there is much more that I want to
    value
But you've such hopeful distaste, Misha said
That fear — of an individual's demanding too little of the
    world
I sat in the chair, looking into the mirror
Blind as milk
People believe it still — there's one night in the year, with its
    sides heaving
Lips aloft, speaking
We — seeking safety in creases
There was a metal clock on a shelf close to the ceiling
Seryozha's kiss was only just then breaking

Chapter 163

Let us behave
I am getting to be
So I can't escape reality
The events are conspicuous but events are not continuous
I behave with improvisation and intention
Minutes, partly
Wings of the homeland
The bicycle rider's backbone
We have a Russian tradition of silence, Dima said
Silence itself, a form but in different locations
I ask for a description of consciousness in a state of silence
For the excitation of Leningrad
This is an eternal nonverity
I am keeping silent now

Chapter 164

Tradition says that Pushkin was a hero and we should pray for
 him
Passion slashed the original
And dear Tolstoi, Dima says — he seems to me to have
 harmfully segregated and isolated his being
What was meant in his place
An old granny is riding the bus with a boy and his head is in a
 glass vase
So, said Vitya, you understand the context in which this is true
The glass is so thick I can't break it, the granny says
And not just between the legs
Besides, we've too much of this symbolic salt and bread
The doctor at the clinic — he gave a monologue like a
 mosquito
He did what death does to life
Isolation can be predicted from a child's memory
But dear lord protect me from an illegible fate
Give me air that splits

Chapter 165

Sleep is a heavy dim medium for dream
White snow and pale yellow pollen on film
The scenes vegetate within their days
We enter
We entertain facing inward
So in Alfred Hitchcock's film about Mayakovsky's life there's a
    scene which opens in yellow and white dawn light with a
    long shot of crows making din outside a shadow
Wouldn't it offend their reason? Shklovsky asks
I know I'm a poet, but for whom should I write?
In another yellow
There's the yellow of deferral and the other yellow
There's a yellow of nostalgia and of claustrophobia
A fly passes but I can't hit it
There's a red and black of irony, of memory
The monumental stone sphere, eroded by long necessary
    exposure to light, is balanced along the balustrade of the
    strollers' enclave, where the frozen band of the Neva
    reaches — the sphere the enormous condensation of a
    conduit

Heaven is near, but not to the objects we see
It is hardly whole
Restraints, refrains
The sky is in the sun which floods society
It is not sexually innocent — its spittle forms a heaven
Life goes — by sex for shadow
The mouth is frost
It opens to recognize — too brief a loss
The city is a mirror tilted to companionship
Neither women nor men look back
Let's surrender out
Such is a scene again
Several, conspicuous, such — my ice
My inside out

Chapter 167

Why did I read the whole book so quickly
It is a sheep thriller, Arkadii said
Ruthless, untroubled, maudlin, unyielding instincts
A detective novel is very optimistic — it is all about
    construction
Dostoevsky and the deservedness of people
Their responsibilities are always briefly deferred
Ostap said it was a true story of the old granny nailed to her
    head
It's possible
In old people the skull thickens and there is room for such a
    nail
Space is only minuteness, he said, and indecent songs
Notes passed up long paper tubes between women and men
From facing wings of the prison the prisoners pass strings
    through them weighted with balls of bread
What do they say
Obscurity is cruel literary romanticism compared to the
    monstrous obscenity of those great Russian love songs,
    Arkadii said

Chapter 168

In the night I experienced fierce itching in ear
A sleeping that I squirmed to reach
KGB?
Too romantic
But I would nonetheless not speak English even there
A high bird recognition
It was not the telephone ringing
Neither would I speak Russian
Yesterday's hat was my ceiling — not to be confused with
    religion
Music is not to be charged with prayer
What do women want is not to say what do women seek
Yesterday benefited
But beauty is often confused — to discover in the moist
    elaborate detail
Beauty is meticulous but profuse

Chapter 169

The eye is short to sharp memory
I myself sleep at a horizon
The words are like drops in long rains
Flashing and rolling
I cannot quote, I cannot get context
But today, on the 18th of the month, a vast transparent cold
    seemed at times to be drifting down out of the sky or at
    times instead to be pressing up from the frozen ground
    toward it
There was no describing horizon
No foreground and no hierarchy
A quiet protective silver-blue light was shielding the laughter of
    some children who were dragging a sled like a dirty
    bundle through the gray-green slush toward a slope worn
    almost bare between some beaten birches
Tarkovsky's film, Alyosha said
We see from a distance some production of an aesthetic
    apparat
Bright but submerging
There is nothing to demarcate but all is indivisibly precise
Noises fall and nothing denies them

Chapter 170

There's a thick film of ice on the window at which the light
    wobbles
The light whole
My language is an X turning in the hands of two clocks on a
    face over the eye
It rotates until reality comes up
Experiences can only take the indirect responsibility for art,
    Natasha said
Russians do not bind themselves to observation
And, Vitenka, think of the names
Not in the kitchen, Zina said — she was holding a chicken over
    the flame
I think we will have St. Petersburg again and poor Ulianov will
    be buried here or there
Interference and eating — it's the theory and practice of
    writing
One cannot be in a flare or a sorrowful hurry
I don't like this religion of nations, Natasha said
I'm a Jew and that means no nation
So much free will, Vitya said, and so much determinism

Chapter 171

The hunt must accomplish necessity
Then the hunt goes on
The hunt goes one
It widens on the frozen streets
We're made a mother, our influence sweeps, we can draft our
    opinions of poverty
If one doesn't isolate the idea of self, one doesn't experience
    brevity
Brevity wasn't Gogol's fear
Nor Dostoevsky's, though his senses in event occurred from
    many interruptions
Such hunger is more memory than disappointment
Such is our friendship with events
We have words, and their things must remain in abeyance
In current
The shoppers dive — and I follow Zina
Zina arrives with two chickens

Necessities are only links in the interlude
A person's footsteps follow, themselves longing for sleep
For color
Under filthy grass and broken ice pink without interlude
We accept tradition as if it were a reflection of our odd world
    but it's not, Volodia said, it's not
Thuds, pleasures, snow, timidity, telephones — Rosa
    telephoned
Gavronsky was displaced but wasn't dead
There was a scientist from Novosibirsk with no name there,
    working on superconductivity in secret
Time is energy, he said
We work days and nights without sleep and then as now it is
    odd and we take our leave
We were pressed and shared soup
Time is strength
That is a great Siberian soup, the scientist said, the soup of
    strength
We are afraid of space

Chapter 173

There is a full lip at the term of the object of self
What is the precaution, I asked it
An icon, an overlapping
The winter sky was a spread line and growing wider
The colonel slapped his daughter's hand from the ice
Why should I
Where is the hiss of everyday life
A young painter at the Hermitage was copying Titian's
    "Portrait of a Young Painter"
At the Peter-Paul Fortress sunners stood in the sun's line of
    fire
Perfection
Then the young painter pulled a knife
Hillocks, tomatoes, flags, rocks, zebras, a feeling of
    weakness — the fact itself is at its limit
Nature is only some necessary addition to the city
One has merely to lie down and it will pass by

Chapter 174

Nausea falls
But what is consciousness of one's own digestion
Intelligence is a necessary accumulation emitting deep
    philosophical explanations of the love scenes
Revolution
And the colonel began to drink it at once, turning red and
    beginning to perspire
I am a solid citizen and I will surround my own bones
Expanding expanse
The seeing of flesh in its skin
Memory is a soul in boots
No, no, he said — I remember the fifties — the terrible winters
    and broths of boots
The ashes crack
There are no bras in sex scenes without genitals, only breasts
A great encyclopedia lies open to the breast
I pressed it to a tea cup

Chapter 175

There was an eye on each breast, and it was unlidded at night
Their ruthlessness was apparent
The next morning Zina said, "I was dreaming of chickens,"
     and I went along
Flat boots, men seeping in fur hats, two girls to follow
A Soviet collie accompanied a granny dragging a rope
We passed a bathtub against a birch
Mnemonic devices for the Cyrillic
So — it confirms my belief, Vitya said; things indeed exist in
     the world, but they are dispersed over the noosphere
Disproportion, discontinuity, ignorance, sameness, irrelevance,
     oblivion — all the forms of wariness guide us
There was green ice under foot and rock in the sky — and
     without achieving speed
The sun a driven nail
The sun scratching the light
Our modernization couldn't crush the hieroglyphicity of our
     life
Each eye a driven night

Chapter 176

Clarity shelling
I can be culminating but only repeatedly
Our humidity is very gratifying since thanks to it we feel the
    seasons heavily, Alyessa said
But now, Lyn, goodbye, she said, in America I want to see sex
    films
Well, my civilization is willing
Two ruts
And what
And all that they could include
The shell of mist
A mist so tinted that the ice can't get through
It's a face from which the pronoun is missing
I am not I, said a chalk on a wall
Dickface, said a paint on a door close to cozy
I adore you, my cunt, said Dmitrii in English

Chapter 177

In the Hermitage there was no coffee
Cunt of weakness! an American mumbled carefully, reading
    transliteration from a handy traveller's book
There was an original resemblance and the young painter
    slashed it
No coffee, no cold, no hole in this reality, Liuda said
We had descended — tea must be without feminism
It was a terrible thing — a great separation — this young
    painter's knife had a butterfly's wings
But it is our feminism to recall the village, Liuda said
A very strong life — a very strong indication
The smell of spring flooding over the smell of smoke
And fleas? I asked — we have a multitude of fleas
Only berries, dust, dusting, and snow
Peas
And a German drowning herself with a knife
We saw, Liuda said, that nature doesn't seal

Chapter 178

I dreamed that we stood up or crouched down on the same
    spot of ground
It's for luck, Zina explained
If your left palm itches, this means money is coming, but it
    won't be delivered unless you scratch your hand with your
    chin
I'm getting old, Natasha said
She lifted her shirt
I have a son and many breasts but they are hanging
So now I can make only a monotonous exaggeration
Natasha! I said — we must all go to France!
French women are psychologically in society
But such a separation of facts?
There's a shortage of paper — of identification
Okay — how do we resemble
As for me, in sleep I'm a remainder of the world and there are
    walls between the legs
Or maybe eggs and culling

Chapter 179

There is an hour which is an overcoming afternoon
Pictures taking light as we went out
My hand where I had embarrassed it was inflamed
The heel of my boot was coming apart
In the center around the hotel were whores of cement
     silhouetted against lemon odors
Some kind of visa like a pin was accomplished
Swamps and the outskirts of inner weight holding housing
     blocks — there is no way to imagine the flat of home
But at home I often sit on the page done in a whisper
It's impersonal
But don't I aspire to have a strong impersonality
Would when, would where, would what — on a cord in the
     corner of the kitchen
A transparent body of dishes
On a shelf near the ceiling stood a porcelain urn
And walking handles

Chapter 180

Alyessa weeps delicacies, Zina said in the light, sewing a rip in
    the seam of the leg of the jeans Arkadii wore as he stood
    there
By moving a drawer we could open the wine
Strawberries, fire, a very vague death, oily water, the birch
    forest, tiny bluish spiders, carefully hidden windshield
    wipers, a crow, the name of the driver (Alexeyev), and the
    grave of Lenin's mother
It's impossible to telephone Leningrad
Lyn, Vasya said, there are new lines through Helsinki — you
    can call as a business man
It's only plumbing, Arkadii said
My grandmother placing her mouth to her mud
And the daughter of my father
Stones out of dreams
For a long time I couldn't guess whom I resembled
Just the waiting could make me nauseous
Do you agree?
Of course I agreed
I was already breathing

Book Six

Chapter 181

Observations that days come, arrive, approach, are blots,
    hangovers, reactionary reactions, said the doorkeeper at
    the Writers Union on Voinova
The future can't be made out with such metaphors, he added,
    tapping a new tabloid
So, it is my right to present this to an American
Plumbers' beauties are plumbers' proofs
And so, our new poets in leather jackets won't get wet
Only our cheerful tongues
Upstairs I met with Evgenii Ivanovich, who was translating the
    American metaphorist Raymond Chandler
A pale man with a tiny pad
He turned away and lifted its page
What does it mean, please, "The woman had rubber lips with
    no tread"
She's lost her grip on the truth
Or maybe what she says goes by him
We have no such metaphors, he said, but maybe I'll find one
Maybe something like, "The circle she made with her mouth
    was warped"

Chapter 182

The women in the restaurant blew out battered rings of smoke
They're typical, said Natasha, of our bureaucrats working in
    offices guarded by office rats
Not only that but this
But I was a mere observer at my vanishing post
A perceiver pressed between several young girls who were
    eating cakes and glancing at my coat
I rested my cup on the ledge provided not far from the
    door — a regular spot
Katya blew when I laughed at Arkadii
The coffee's too hot
Such bureaucrats pretend to be discreet but they are merely
    banal
They very carefully oblige
And you
We oblige in return
Returnedness is a mighty abstraction, ring within ring
That's how we really remember

Chapter 183

It's a woman's fate to forecast the future in sex
The word itself, sex, is a hole in the body of death
Patience is passion
And passion denied
A photo and floral blotches on the wall
The window was open and the blanket fluttered
I was stark as in Bergman's "Persona"
I was turned over
That was the most terrifying confusion in art, I said
A true confession I guess in a religious glass
Like voyeurism in the dead's edge of the Russian church
Women had been sighing like whales
In the open coffin neither man nor woman
Neither open

Chapter 184

Beside the Summer Garden, Vanya was expressing eternal
    dissatisfaction

> *My boat drifts away*
> *hardly disturbing*
> *happy ducks dozing*
> *on the cracking mud*

There was yellow on the Moika
And a deep terra cotta glow on the Mikhailovsky Palace
Mayakovsky, if for the good of the revolution you were
    required to write iambic verse, would you?
They asked him that

> *I went to the fruit shop*
> *There were no bananas*
> *There was only you*
> *And an ugly brown dog*
>
> *The dog made a sound*
> *The fruit flies were quiet*
> *The majority hears it now*
> *The majority says it's real*

But, said Vanya, weaving a little, we've encountered a little
    break in the supply supply
Still, a purchaser is never free
Right?
Right?
I don't like Mayakovsky

If you've too much of it, the next day you feel remorse
Or else you get used eventually to everything
So I drift away waving my boat
He waved his boot

Chapter 185

If a person is killed for revenge, it's murder not assassination
And murder sanctioned is execution
Or war
Stains in the dark, voices in drawers, a figure strolling over the
    bed who says no
And a rolling head
Means mean beliefs
The Russian in a man's description
Ghosts go to the sides, so that days seem not to be filled
Cadets crowded the Nevsky sprinting a curve toward the
    obscenity course
All their desires are equal, Mitya observed
A group of soldiers was pointed toward a gap in a restaurant
The wedge reinforced
The slapping bedded
Life never led them, the grannies say, but life is life

Discontinuity is self-contained — that's an effect of
    nationalities
But an idea is not ours
Nor while moving certainly, absolute
A horde, and I had to admit that I wasn't an occupant
But the doorman permitted me, after an argument, to come in
Why not — he shook my hand
Mayakovsky, he said
I knew the marvel, the state of being hard to know
The witness was expressionless
Or its love is
We never remember
Whittling dry mud, watching a detachment run
I had thought of something impervious, something experience
But that too, for the moment, I forgot

Chapter 187

Most days and nights there was no particular point and so no
    direction from there
I could only move, even naming in place
Probably that's why I couldn't sleep — I was always sleeping
    away
Then we often ate no matter how late
Noodles, soft scallions, and salt
Pickled stalks
I wandered in trust with nothing to tell
Nothing, but it wanted its figurative form
Just time in the kitchen with spoons, flames, and steams
Nobody's business, nobody's narration
We just scurried in our socks
We could only have pleasure as we changed
But I wondered if it was rude to read the dictionary then
And it was always more different in the morning

Chapter 188

What is the scope of the experience of sex — we talked about
    that
The crowding it forecasts
A poise pitching
Or the incompetence — it's as if you're trying to find the way
    around another woman's kitchen
Or man's — but that's too much
Proprietors of our own mud and flour
Rain was falling, dividing the light
It was he who was plunging, Masha said, how could I stop
Life always attracts attention
And the trees bristle
The tree tries to remain in one spot with innumerable
    gradations
So sex just condenses disorientation
Then there's jealousy, that crazy bridge
But do not compare, Arkadii said, living is incomparable

Chapter 189

Sasha Gavronsky was exhibiting his works in an abandoned flat
    in a condemned building
In the seven sinks of the once communal flat he was floating
    varnished newspaper boats
On the seven rims he'd stenciled the word vanished in English
I'm unambiguously unserious, he said, like a fanatic who can't
    believe God
A graffiti green Satan cuddling a puppy and Jesus with ice
    cream in two squares between broad cross-hatchings
Katya was playing with her son in a corner, whom she had
    home for a few days from her mother
He makes youthful gestures, Lyosha said
Why not! he's a youth
I like him, Zina said — he has a memory with sweetness and
    you watch, his eyes seem small but he's thinking about
    everything
A kid in a suit was watching the crowd
He calls himself Leo — the first Soviet Castelli
He controls this flat
He says he's supporting the painters of the heavy mental
He's announced their movement as "the art of Mordredism" in
    some article

Chapter 190

I'd been so long from my sources of news that I felt somewhat
    left out of history
Zina also likes to watch news
Banging the tidings, booming the mind
Impossibility is exhausted
I quoted — it makes me feel old and fresh
Hidden mind and forecast reason and brandished mention
Boom and a nail of thought is driven into a board of reason
I don't know what to think
I think of what I want to know
Meat sought below holes in the snow
Hoops of desire are spun around reason
Secrecy is impossible — so is synopsis
The sum of six hundred seconds
Ostap laughed — so now we have proved flying sausages

Chapter 191

Where does Grisha get his money?
Grisha has no money
He has his intention, his assurance, his connection
He's Russian
And in a further fascination which is at art and nature
Nothing is ever needed, since everything can change
Maybe he leaves home in the morning but maybe he comes
    home then too
There's nothing about money in such accounts
Maybe a skylark and an army truck
A clever but not audacious ram
History is more cautious
But can you say it's constant
From time to time but not from place to place
Or point to point

Chapter 192

But to return to the theme of the novel and poetry
That is, one theme
The time comes when each individual poem reveals not only
    its own internal connections but also spreads them out
    externally, anticipating the integrity each poem requires
    in order to explain obscure points, arbitrary elements,
    etc., which, if they were kept within the limits of the given
    text, would seem otherwise to be mere examples of the
    freedom of expression
One can't be intimidated by the threat of subordination
Nor by petty attractions nor semantic conflicts
By poplar fluff and Chinese islands
And not even by compositional imperatives demanding new
    texts
But there are days — let's not forget real days — when
    language loses speed
Then it lags as the nights lag, brief and nonetheless long
And one submits to a sensation
It's something entirely meaningless and unexpected
It's devoid of interpretation, a perfect quiddity
The long awaited meeting of signifier and signified
And one begins to examine the construction of small
    resonating forms (this occurs most often in spring), to
    investigate their behavior, and to extract from that a set of
    — I couldn't say images — principles which seem to be
    the only ones adequate to the attempt *to say nothing*

Chapter 193

Evgeny Onegin is a novel of manners (Belinsky called it
   encyclopedic), a family saga, an autobiography, an aimless
   plot with the symmetry of time, an impression of
   philosophy, and *Dead Souls* is an epic, hopeful of
   resurrection
The epic, said Mikhail Kheraskov, will remember important,
   memorable, famous events occurring in this world to
   cause important change, or it will sing of events occurring
   in a certain state to glorify life, or occasion peace, or
   finally, to provoke a transition to a different condition
The red nosing of frost, rumors of cheese and deploying the
   hunt, two colonels on the night before Lent rending a
   tough goose, etc., against the crushing of the Neva
Every fact could break through deterministic constraints
What of a conflict between a person's inner world and the
   environment
But no, one turns out and the other in and conflict is resolved
   into vertigoes and spun on perpendiculars
They coincide — not in the grapefruit (it comes from
   Havana), nor in tight apples (from Pushkin), but in a
   collie (evoking irrational fears)
A familiar organism, the alienating device
Equally marvelous, as Gogol said, are the lenses that
   contemplate a star and those that study a bug
Everyone has to eat and many eat potatoes, but some of those
   also eat pineapples
Tarasov says the pineapples are enormous in Siberia
Like literary reminiscences
Like two squirrels playing on a tree
Like heroes of a picaresque novel without separable facts

Chapter 194

So, said Evgenii Ivanovich, I understand
"The woman had loose lips and I was sick of hearing them
    flap"
It is derogatory, she is too fat, I know Americans are afraid of
    fat
But you know our Russian peasant's compliment to his wife
In the morning before I left home I slapped her on the ass and
    at night when I returned the ass was still shaking
But in the city version of our story, he said, she talks too much
Always out with friends all standing in a row against a wall to
    benefit from the light which travels sideways from the sun
    on the perpetual horizon
But it's a problem of perceivers whose perceptions can't be
    tied
But, if you don't mind, could you explain for me the symbolic
    meaning of the name of your beverage *Johnny Walker*
Also, Marlowe, am I right, suggests the idea "more law," which
    in Russian is *bol'shye zakon*
Well, so, my Marlowe is called Zabolkonsky
I do not want to drop any California ideas
This is the place to keep them
Like a spoonful of jelly in my tea

Chapter 195

Tomorrow is the only sense of finishing I get
An armload of potatoes, some decisive steps
Why do you make a martial song in a flute's tones, Derzhavin
    himself asked
Love is interference, jealousy the guard
To put it more convincingly he touched his thumb tip to the
    tip of his forefinger, stuck the circle into his mouth, and
    produced a whistle as piercing as a needle
He followed it with a melodious warbling trill
Later this would stretch my dreaming of daylight
The highway adapted to expectations
A battered tricycle, boys with their hands tied by scarves
What do you hear of Salik, I asked
He's gone back to Uzbekistan full-throated
Like a great cat in a verb of reserve
Or a butterfly in an accident of belief
His guests all nod

Chapter 196

Can one ever not be surprised by war
How it follows its usefulness and fouls it
The dark Kazan Cathedral lay around war poets on crutches
Iraq, Iran, Ethiopia, Afghanistan
Their blasts abashed
We cannot give them
The soldiers no longer live them
The burns fall
A bird climbs from a pocket
There's no middle
The edge is gathering to go back
Soldiers wallow over wonder
Citizens in clusters to show it
War and no one to know it

Chapter 197

Vasya had his brother's winter coat
He was taken, Misha said, from village prose
Heavy as felt
Harassed
Can you imagine being able to cheat like that
By mistake he carried the gun himself, which made him grow
    more and more angry
Such dense heat rolled from his stomach that he couldn't see a
    thing around it
At night he was silent and drank clay
The wool still smelled wet
My brother at that time was a spiritual man with a personal
    body, said Vasya
Well, and then
First he tried to cut off his hand
And then
Well, he was shot by a colonel in the spine

Chapter 198

Misha!
Ho!
Give Lyn more tea
It's an exercise of free will to improve the world, Misha said
One corner of the table was supported by books
Alyessa added tea
I'm already postfeminist, she said
Misha's geranium stood by the bed
Five leaves and a bud on a meter of trunk
Its simple being isn't lost, Misha said, but its complexities seem
    to have fallen off
With one like that you have a table leg
Ira propped more paintings against the wall
A house like a hole and two women on an orange cow
They will never go West — I refuse it, she said

A banded vase behind a wall of paint crushing a face
Ira showed three panels, iconlike, scenes of a sugar cube,
    sunflower shells, and trucks in a field behind pounded
    scrap metal from the street
Perhaps satiric, Misha said
I don't think so, Ira said
Two orange cows afloat above and pulling a boat into a brown
    and yellow sky
Not sky
The interior without walls but very close
A green of terrible globs encircled by a continuous parade
Ira laughed — there's the colonel with his baby in a pram in
    the snow
A woman sweeper, a man in medals
A woman in medals
The survivors of the siege of Leningrad
And here's our Lenin — I inserted a lump of wax
What did Lenin want

Chapter 200

In the foyer outside *OVIR* hung a painting (in the style of
    Renoir) of Lenin in springtime emerging from a tide in
    his suit, like an emerging stage of consciousness
A waiting produced by motion
Evgenii Ivanovich had raised both his hands — *OVIR* is the
    frog's leap from a phone booth
Now night had come early, with flickering phosphors
Do you know what we say of a clever girl?
She has her own butter in her head
It has stirred
And of a crazy man, that his roof has moved
I thought I smelled of cigarettes and dirty hair
Of airplanes
But everything so slowly matters
And the hours at *OVIR* entirely filled the place
I am quite comfortable, I said
Then I will smoke just past the door, Arkadii said

Chapter 201

The compassionate passions are the wandering ones
Out the door, out the roof — or a number of roofs (but we
    were on the top floor)
I imagined it as a face applied and to that a face complied
No lack of force to a board of the bus
A heavy bag on a stranger's lap
But recently there've been outbreaks of screaming
"Pull your frog's legs back under your stump," and so forth
A woman in a bonnet of chemically orange fur
Modistka, Zina whispered
She has a head you can't pity because it's one without profile
The yellow wind sank to the floorboards
I pressed two tissue tickets past me to the punch
I had made this mobility, punctured to the month
But maybe my intentions were immobilized to go

Chapter 202

The standing things along the Neva fell by light
I had a strong feeling, as if film were there, of black and white
The Neva groaned where the water flowed
A yellow tug crackled and icicles hung from the metal tendrils
    of all that was most
A silence keeping to itself encrusted trucks
A film of battleships — or no, a room
That was the thing
What is a thing
By thing I mean object, subject, event, scene, situation, or even
    milieu, like the numbers 202 or 17, as when we say, the
    thing is January will be cold, or, it's a good thing I have a
    map
There's nowhere to get lost — or no, there's nowhere to be
    found
But Zina wanted me to know a place
She meant, for example, my bed for the best
A place to hear between
A place to unframe

Chapter 203

A chipped flange on the dangling pipe bringing in our
        cooking gas
It's in a prepositional state — for, not for, off, on
What can we say of individualism? of cells?
That is just my way
A woman had been struck in a zebra and killed
The driver clung
She was nowhere — how could I stop
Traffic lights broken, ice on the street
He's technically guilty unless she was drunk
It's five, seven years, after such an event
And events happen, but this doesn't have to mean that
        another event has happened before
Habits before — the favorite cup
Horses that have freed themselves
I think I should get up and chase them

Chapter 204

Dima arrived a little damp as if he'd run
The Soviet army was close on Slava
So Slava was practicing for seizures
You have to imagine ice, Liuba said
No, Mama, I have forgotten all that, of course, pounding his
     head
I wave my hand and yellow eyes blink
I'm a capsized vessel sinking in the dreamy deeps
But my soul had insomnia and departed
Maybe for Africa — I don't know — it escaped
It feels everything, that's why it's suspicious
It's as Sinyavsky said it is, that soul's a shapeless patriot
A cabbage
Then one night the polyclinic called — it was time
And case

Chapter 205

My genre cannot share the darkness, not with mixed
    allegiance
There are prepositions everywhere in the possessive
The of of one and the of of all, a difference to infinity
Obscenities (there's no cause for direction), the saturation of
    real events, talk of the death of abstractions observed,
    patterns with no position, an old man selling off a bronze
    lantern shaded in silk
There's a pinpoint in which the boundaries end
A mere speck between public and private, said Boris Vodonoy
The speck a seed
That must produce a boundary problem
People feeling without bends, unconfined
It's nothing (coming) to be deferred
And anything, too — spreading around, like the forced air
    warming the night
Assertive and disinclined
The problem of personal hours, however, could certainly be
    solved
Of what I am certain

Chapter 206

Police from crime had closed the street
I don't understand how they prove innocence
The anonymity of innocence
People make confessions of innocence
Situations requiring repairs to the state of affairs
A person can't activate a window
A window in its ideal idleness had provoked a crowd to smash it
But nothing was divided
We feed our violence to the clean contemplations
The window was not a limit
The window wasn't transparent — it had served our need of link
Our animosity for time and place
The handshake between them had not been made
The city cinemas

Chapter 207

The size of the hour doesn't matter, no more than the size of
    the torso
The sofa could be folded out and sentimentalized
It stood in a corner out of the window, padded when extended
The pillows in collapsed moss points
Like the size of something lunar — a borzoi
I'd seen the borzoi with a woman who held her shawl off her
    medals — herself a colonel
A dim forgotten fear provoked by envelopes
And the taste of the sheet on dry teeth
The water first in a concentrate, then water raised
The strata soaking in
Water never bothers the look because it cups its continuity
And the size of the river doesn't bother
The Neva itself was at once involving
Looking down the shadow sentence shapes elongate

Chapter 208

Vladimir Nabokov had been in a dream discovered by Kolya
He had turned it up in the Composers Union in the archive
    above a pipe
He hated music — no signs of life
Lydia Yakovlevna appeared to listen, though closely pulling
    flesh off the tiny bones of a fish
She washed the egg in her mouth
A dream must be a fully conscious affair — an exemplum of
    prose
Not a blind spot or an accidental drowning
A radish exploded
And the lingonberries prevented pneumonia
Books usually seek, Lydia said
A dream has no position after itself, only its own position
Well, Lydia, Kolya said, pressing the fish into the bread, he was
    very positive and even offered to pay for the room while
    awaiting the mail
That's real enough, in any case, no rubles in the middle but
    crumbs to begin and end
She rose very slowly — I know you're teasing, Kolya — the
    mail's much more dependable than the telephone

Chapter 209

Arkadii, I complained, this is like chipping with an axis
Nothing but spindles and needles to waver
And conjunctions to slide, ring within ring of coinciding
      wobbling borderlines
Here's a landscape drawn in a quandary for children
Things in the picture are hidden but once found one can
        never not see them though to someone who's never
        looked they're still out of sight, lost in the lines
Outside in the park a child hung on the slope suspended on a
      sled that wouldn't slide
Lyosha laughed — it's just a gullible child
As I, he added
A normal intermittent ride
He'll divide it, or try further to the side, as just here in this part
      of the window
There we make his solitude
Nothing but spans and nodules to feature
And corners to transpose, wire along wire, alien to a landscape
      of tips
A push to what it contains

Chapter 210

The hysteria was static, within a transmission
A love of small life
A flicker in transition
Or the woman who was mesmerized and a dolphin in the
women's bath
For three days she would not interrupt the likeness
What happened, I asked
For this they brought the hypnotist
Bound to necessity means bound to unlikeness
Our Russian kindness
The third embankment
Tasting questions
Rushing chapters
Later the woman was muffled in amazement
Existence *is* direction

Chapter 211

The night Gavronsky was attacked there'd been wind but no
    more than plaster tick
Or plaster fall
The bell on the flat was wadded with a hat
There were conversations more loud than mean as one needs
    to be
Like canvas flapping
A projector fan
A snowball slid against the kitchen window
Katya banged empty bottles onto the balcony
Seryozha danced and a neighbor complained
The Architects Union was closed
At night it was easier to know it as Nabokov's street
Or to know it as anyone else's street
It hadn't been history's but the navy's or the sea's
And then a separation

Alienation is a condition of utmost duality
In this it resembles solitude
The simultaneous assertion and negation of one
Solitude gives one the feeling of everything's spaciousness,
     including that of reason, to which repetitions are never
     only repetitions, but insist on change
But alienation insists that this life is something you yourself
     haven't experienced
Or anything rushes into the eyes whenever it's given a chance,
     freeing anything from everything, isolating the minutest
     facts
So between phrases it's essential that other phrases be
     inserted, and that they intercede logically, so the world
     will gain stability and the writer won't seem like an idiot
Sincerity under such conditions is subordinate to perception,
     even to perceptions I can't accept
These conditions are nothing necessitated
And nothing needed
Slipping provided
And intercessions still enlivened
What I understood was still only the tightest oscillation
And seeing some things never move at all

Chapter 213

Something serves to smolder in the sound of any night
The birch leaves were hissing, a nightbird was flapping its
    wings
Water thudded along the embankment and somewhere a wire
    whined
The thrumming of conversations rose through the walls, with
    the merging of consonants and singing of vowels
A single car cuckooed in the dark
The rustling of the sweater taken off, the shuffling of socks on
    the floor
Misha popped a cork down the throat of the wine
So, and well, as you say — being!
And its gurgle inscribed
May its dots scratch the paper when you open your book
Zina lit a candle — it spluttered like spilling rice
Once she rose to get water and the stream banged a pot
I could hear my tongue clasp my mouth as I yawned
The candle flickered like one of the nasal stars

The wind is the idle herald that mercury provides
The star (golden whistle), the painter (conversing citizen), the
    observer (with no native ease)
A spirit of time (of varying lengths), an orange geiger counter
There's an art to the factory whistle, a future for the bell, good
    intentions, numbers, a sword in the house of art
My purse is a continent, a conduit for compassions
Syntax set on scales, a wait for judges, flames (bog fires)
The morning lights are order posts
Life (busy willfulness) must be applied
A small dawn (slow combinations), a satyricon, an irritable slav
    (in the end unharmed)
The useful East, the useful West — these are suitably flat
    progressions
Ellipses
We and time, but no opposites, so no tautologies
Sucking what we survey (sweet garlic) with other summers
    (questions of life), we conduct quick transitions
A gust (in the lock), a writer (held in prose), settled in

Chapter 215

Despite obvious watchers, despite consciousness, there were
    times in every terminus
The montage can only be made
We'd taken a trolley made solely of soft metal junctures on
    mercury hinges
In the back were two kids
All the kids have number tendencies to reject nothing
Rubber plugs and the right to drive tourists
The paper shine in a zone of commission
It's number, why could there be quality
Like Zapinsky, he's famous since Sotheby's — they want a
    color off his line
They are the twist to get the shed off every supply
It's dangerous breathing in forks of this kind
Or maybe it's just first breezes
Something as nebulous as an epigram
Something as prophetic as a last line

Chapter 216

The mercury measure
The mercury rolling note
And another — with a German melting lead to cast fortunes
A post-Marxist, he said, dripping sand
A steel bar across the restaurant door
Kuryokhin was playing a concert at the Palace of the Culture of
    Trade Unions
Every concert is silent of something, Sergei said, but not mine
Because I'm jealous, not political
The music is like Derzhavin's "Ode to Fortune," made "when
    the author in person was tipsy"
Owed to an auspicious state
Maybe he said I want to be like a man in a dining car
Or maybe like a child riding a Great Dane
Spilled
Contained

Chapter 217

Recognition in itself is a source of great excitement
I discovered I knew *Tekhnologicheskii Institut* as well as *Ploshad*
　　Lenina
Deductions are directions
Truths change, things develop
I felt a thrill of gratitude — to whom or what it may refer
Lurking with competence, I was familiar with the future
It was humid, and the air smelled of crystal bog fires
A pastel slick, artist unknown, was distending the truth of the
　　canal
The layer always existing between day and night
That's our mother-of-pearl, Ostap said, waiting on the corner I
　　recognized
Are there environmentalists
Oh!
Maybe so
They want to save Petersburg from Jews

Chapter 218

The numbers of memory have never been totalled
It's said they're going home, and it's said they're empty
But someone had developed the *glasnost* metaphor: open and
    let something out
Maybe later, Ostap said
At the moment the cold wind was yellow
Two figures on motorcycles going different directions on a
    Prussian blue road fading to black having already passed,
    factory chimneys on the right, snow and bare trees, the
    closer in goggles, the other only a back
A painting of language, he said with a laugh — I'll call it,
    Paragraph
And here, *The Descending Idea*, and *Landscape No. 1* and also
    Landscape No. 1
Then a view of a courtyard and a table on a truck only half
    through the arch in a courtyard with a woman, her head
    thrown back, ignoring a pigeon on the ground
Retreat to the Dacha?
No, *People Will Surrender Even Their Spoons for Fear A Magnet Will
Discover What They've Hidden*
And this is *Portrait of a Moscow Poet* — he can't drink because of
    a wound to his head
The water had come to a boil in the kettle
I moved a painting aside

The Oedipus act is accomplished
Now an idea crosses an insatiable hunger for tangibility
The trajectories of a thousand necessities tangle
A bee, attracted to its own honey, falls onto the table
A pool of tea reflects the blue sun
Tiny tears in the ocher curtain release ants of light onto the
    floor
The stove is silent
Now and then some mechanism hisses inside the toilet
Arkadii briefly sucks the tip of his finger pricked by a brass
    filament bristling from the cord with which he's going to
    rewire the phone
The silence is broken by scissors
The blue bindings of Blok's works have faded
The drying shirts outside the window have flattened into
    frozen pads
I think of the crows in the snow and the cliche that rhymes
    snows with rose
Not only imagination sustains the intransitive activity of
    anticipation

Khlebnikov proposed that we "construct the art of waking up
    easily from dreams"
He also suggested a rule of monuments
A person's birthplace and a person's monument should stand
    at precisely opposite spots on the globe
There should also be "running and traveling monuments"
    erected on pickup trucks or on flatcars on trains
Misha moved out of the sunlight and complained that his head
    ached
You must believe that I'm lazy, he said
I can't make anything out of my dreams — they simply deposit
    themselves, each one in the next
A banal fate
Everything surrounds it and nothing sticks up
But there are no gaps in my laziness, and for that reason I can
    work
The huts harboring statues in the Summer Garden were being
    dismantled
There'd been a great scandal some months before
Rumors of a bomb dropped in the 40s and unexploded under
    one of the paths
They dug a great hole with nothing in it

Chapter 221

There were fears in the 40s of attack on California, I said
I've been told that my grandmother decided we should go out
    of the city
And we did so, to a place a few hours south
The only place on the continent that received a Japanese shell,
    as it turned out
And?
The same — it too never exploded
Then Arkadii was born at random in Potsdam
Arrivals and departures are often that way, not indicative of the
    siege in the middle
The sitting, the willing, the dividing that never gets finite
Our fathers were colonels
But one can separate that
Stars and alarms
With the apathy to name
The free will nationalists

Chapter 222

The sofa was a nearly dark tank
Above was the face of a horse who'd just drunk
And I couldn't remember Lunacharsky's patronymic
Born in Poltava, "red star of pluralism," poppies without such
    words
The first thing he did was to ask for an aspirin
Just one
The limbs seemed swollen by nettles
Across a cultivated marsh, just on the other side of the river, a
    bell without clapper swung at the monastery
Ostap went to the ambulance
The light shone on the domes
A woman from KGB with some geese socked a hoe into the
    mud
At the signal the horse was dry
Heroes but not purists, Lunacharsky said
Causes with the oldness to think

Chapter 223

A fierce wind was humiliating all who went out in the
    provinces
Blue wolves whispered near the bus stop
The Neva splashed everywhere
It was hard to muffle
We were arm in arm
There's an infinite line in Moscow, Masha said, waiting — it's
    completely indifferent and terrifying — to enter
    McDonald's
And meanwhile people are turning to chalk in the cold
Have you been there?
It's expensive
Everyone's crazy
Burger!
It's just cutlets!
Maybe a different language but the Americans are fascinating
    because everywhere they can make their same meat
So, they make it in Russia and Russians wait to know if it's truly
    the same

Chapter 224

I never seemed fated to be in Russia nor reviewing for patterns
    that prove prophetic
Memories established other matters — irrevocability
Our coincidences weren't sublime departures — all the more
    reason to go
It was awkward but I wasn't afraid
Passing messages down breaded threads with very little to say
Going any place in that ambient destination
But that's not all one
And not intimate to thought so not line but light
Apple-like
In apple-like divisions
With old apple orders
Specifically
Odors and colors are precise not approximations
The unfated opened and answered to apple

Chapter 225

They say in this city there's a pathos of space
That over the life there has never been closure
The chances of closure, the afterward of closure
Maybe something off-limit but not so desirable
Not even the concealing of closure
Maybe a tiny point, a prick of likeness
But comparisons frequently separate what's identifiable
Like poplar fluff from snowflakes, they are only an irony
And there is nothing fateful in the crow to the snow
Although the crows are going to keep it
They'd differed the dogs and driven them out
A fascination for closure, several violent clockwise closures
Paths through the neighborhood crossing closures
At the end of one near a bathtub of thawing mud the neighbor
    with the collie was standing near a car and staring in again
    at its motor

The moment that a knife strikes is not a moment of execution
Do you have the death penalty, I asked
Impossible to imagine it's being seen
Saturated shadows soaking in light
There are worse penalties
For the criminal, yes, but not for the rest
Hanging in the room cold from the floorboards pressed into
    sense of passage
Is it for revenge or for purification, I suppose
For the precision and detail of their intersection
For detachment and inspection
For social abstraction
Slow discussion to correspondence with a life
A moment's notice
It's not completeness of the rest that remains

Chapter 227

The numbers could count every thought by sight
Kids carrying just the edges of razors welded to rings
They wore them palm down within blue tattoos
Just a stroke to the cheek and a face was inscribed
Frost on the sides
A ladder of grammars swinging past
Every thought is the sister of some expression
The chicken
Every word is a process permitting flight
When leaving, for example, we can simply say, farewell, the
     hospitality of your home is great, which we leave now for
     another
Something's possible, but it may be no more than someone's
     asking who's the child of the wife of a cock
Strictly respected and unvarying as content is arbitrary
Sign for disorientation
Crime for orientation

Chapter 228

The sight of sights is influence — I can't refine
I'm always behind
At the edge of a sort of cross-wonder, as if I'd never heard any
    story before
It's not just the stretch of grass but the peasants and the drivers
    out of gas
Generous to a horde, as the grannies would say
Their bench to thrive from
Between the trees the light immured
But the time accumulates, impressionability is tense
Let's say that I'll know where I was, I said
My memory is friendly to all that is personal
The sweet objects of person they hold in their laps
A piece of rope, a door key, a shapka with torn earflaps
Do you think those babushkas smoke
Seen through the blue of a presence we constantly sensed

Chapter 229

I hadn't the sense that I'd acted to be there
It had just been thought, or unseeing stare
Nothing accomplished, nothing managed by a perfectionist
The senses expanded, sensations dropped, and person
        suspended
Sent out
We needed bread, and I'd seen it done — bread-buying filled
        its own system
But for pendulums of cheese one had to be of known origin
One had to know one's point with its powers of extension
From point to line
The many legs of humankind
Well, if you're going to shuffle, then do it where it helps your
        mother, as one of the grannies said
Shifting need to need
Presently
Not with trajectories but with axes

Chapter 230

Memory evokes the anxiety from which living was relieved
Days to be lost in to be found from in the past
The neighbors themselves were little more than pronunciation
One thing in the time of another
Let them think of their own domestic epics, Vitya said
And we wrapped the plates in rags when we took them out
But I thought of them too in the hum without attrition
In the dense ant past
In every oaty summer
For them I always assumed I was reading
Bunching the pages into wedges between my fingers, then
    releasing the batch to subdivide again
Beds from spilled milk, braids from dust, boiling water from
    wind in the poplars
There's a point beyond which memories can't be divided
    further, when one thing becomes another
Now you know where you are, Arkadii would offer

Book Seven

Chapter 231

I was awake after perfect sleep permitting the possibility that its
    listener may not exist
In silence and time bumping
To sit at the window and watch the wind slashing the sheets
Why not invite some friends over and all do laundry late at
    night together until the milky shine of the clothes hangs
    over the billows of dry grass
I'm taking off my wet hat, gluing on an ink beard, and
    warming my hands on the wall, Arkadii said
The cold was noisy
Unlocked
I intended to take up anything
Fantasy, prediction, Pushkin, flats
I should read . . ., I said
Language strengthens the impulse for improvement
And back then death is like magic
It's what sleep is now
Slowly facing and then dissolving the subjectivity with which we
    think we've always been precise

Chapter 232

Not scenes but a science of love disposed
Situations that one can hardly hold
A slow language is a past one, a language of acknowledgment
It would linger experience — I could say such a thing
The often, and the very lack of it
No plot, no hero
Digressions like "there never was . . ." return one to childhood,
    when love was posed by this same state of waiting
Green and yellow in my oftenness, smell of cat, the impress of
    preparedness
Embraces
A state of writing called obsession, history, and prose
Masculine and feminine
Alternating, plain, and crossed
With plausible futures, second smoke
Getting down to the floor in omen

Chapter 233

Every sentence thence is a corridor within a door
Well, something's possible certainly, Lyosha said
A new look at life
But maybe there's no more than a black cat in the bag
Some dramatic insomnia — the simply temporary situation
    and the inexact solace
A Bulgarian refrigerator kept in the bedroom where the carpet
    exploded
An agronomist with a penguin to call Tsar
A journey in the porter's car to Tambov
To Igor the journalist we had tried to explain that life to
    writers is less experimental
I note that you write about sex, he said at last
Things occur with which sometimes one wants to comply
And there are strong complications with the female sex words
Their sentimental sides
The false opposition between inside and out

Chapter 234

I'd asked who was there for adventures so well- taken from
    those who told them
A bell caught on a river — is this a new buttercup
Anything was possible — it had cohesive force
Women wading out every morning to the tops of their thighs
    to restore their life-bearing organs
There was no talk of money, it had no method there
Only secrets of the thumb to every measure
A babushka in a real silk shawl milking straight into a pitcher
I had seen the milk on her leg running
The spinning blue shadow of the goat
Overhead a bio-airplane flew through the milky metal
A region of pure lofty mud
We ran around like rain
We were as serious as an animal
All areas of beauty were the only things we saw

Chapter 235

An August day was pink and brown to press against
Then I was removed
But let us suppose this was not the case
Likeness is not concerned
We were aroused
What lies outside human time, outside the globe of daylight
There are confines to a human life, then a person dies — has
    it lost its life
Life for the exercise of thought and kindness to look past self
    and time
When Pushkin died we remembered it but it lostwhat he
    remembered
Memories and illusions of effect
We should grieve for Pushkin's memories
We were crossing the little beaten forest between the bus stop
    and the housing blocks
Sweetie, said an old woman who stopped as I was passing, I
    haven't smelled a French perfume in forty years
I looked up at a reddish cobalt patch of sky, put my hand on a
    birch with a greasy trunk at a turn on the path

Chapter 236

A sudden summer storm — the thunder-bubbling buckets
    were turned over in the sky
A smell of fruit and diesel rose, the waters swirled
Zina ran to pull the washing from the window sill, throwing it
    back from the rain
Dust from the herbs spun in the air
They were smelling like coffee, then like vinegar
Already the papers were puckered — I kicked at a book
The window was stuck, the curtains flew out
Ostap came in as if he'd walked down the rain
There's so much wind, he said, the rain can't fall
Space eclipsed by speed in no direction, laughter
Foaming parallels
Each strand of rain would slip aside, giving way to another
    coiling down before us
Everyone was feeling glorified, invoked
Water filled inscriptions in the mud

Chapter 237

The petals of the flowers are installments
They follow the potatoes that Arkadii brought home in his
    rucksack
The era of adventure is over, he said, now comes the time for
    venture
Some Volodia had begun a private postal service
Guaranteed delivery of anything within Leningrad in a day
Now he had three hundred messengers
He took a mouthful of parsley head and dill
And he'd cornered some paper
The symbol will be a world and over it a radiant sun
No, we've had enough empires
Something modest — a stroke to represent the horizon bar
Or a common window sill
Zina pulled the horseradish from under the open window
Turn over apple, I will see your other side, she said

Chapter 238

New experiences are wide in a distance, as with time the
     prosaic expands
An automatic apple, steam stoving its light
A sock in its boot, where nothing would collapse it
Romance in a steady sense, pauses
It's because of appearances, passivities, what's in and
     uncommon
And people feeding dogs
Tea and lumps of kasha
Each word germinating to a pelter in its place
The new is the longing of resource
The show of ears
The ground weight
I spent a stride and sheet — the times were not pedantic
What conducted the dilemma of intentions
The submission of possessions

I was spare within times non-parallel
Spatter with proportions
Times parted to anticipate more within
Now the iron was set to heat on the stove, the meat to melt in
    the sink
We had times to prepare — lists, sums, and divisions
But this reads like a manifesto, I said
Find a tincture of nutrition
Get camels' tails of all sizes
Determine the name of the quiet, simple, unsociable yellow
If you can't find that, it's better not to attempt Pushkin
But don't be afraid of small interruptions
All riddles seem too swift in their motion, too compressed in
    their text
Who signs what you see
There's only that imperfect curvature for measuring the
    governments of the earth

Chapter 240

I spoke of rain and received what I spoke of
A continuation of quotations
Misha ate incredibly slowly, as if every bite of mutton soup was
    a test of his honesty
And he returned with manic persistence to the pot as if it
    contained some mystery
Finally he wrapped a piece of bread around a bouquet of
    parsley — a scrap of green wagged at the side of the
    sandwich
They will only accept letters in white envelopes now
That's good, Arkadii said, all my envelopes are white
Literary relics, historical scenes, sea battles can be
    internationally dispersed
Also scientific facts — the things children collect
Sudden American paperbacks
The destruction of the postulates in poetry on which that
    notorious reference depends
I decided to add the following line
My face at the window so unfamiliar it refuses
The refracted phrases as we opened the window to the rain

Chapter 241

Mechnikov speaks only of possible immortality
That leaves us neither in nor out
Like a counterfeiter in prison, a fine description
But is it the time remembered or the memory of time that's
    preserved
It's not immortality but autobiography you mention, said
    Viktor
That was the Mechnikov who attributes our street
Both are intimations of a long wait, an act of deferral
A sex act
Speaking of memory, and of reservation, having no duration
The immortal soul survives but let's say without its
    circumstances
Then, yes, autobiography is more desirable
The Pushkin River flowing into the Sea of Pushkin
Lomonosov into Lomonosov
But autobiography is not monument

Chapter 242

Here's a dacha with a chimney and a man with a tree growing
    from his head
Real lemons appear
And spokes
The lemons are whittled and sprinkled on rice
Everything really happens and its metonyms happen as well
All the acts of a butterfly, all the acts of the canvas sheet, all the
    print acts, the comic boots, the selves bound in bed, the
    poetry strip, the frosted web, the change of attack, and the
    charge of impressions
An ankle in pain means the guest will bring wine
The third bark of the collie means Trotsky won't be revived
An aunt drinking vodka with nothing to eat means Gumilev
    was under the window
A window held open by Dostoevsky on the sill means the
    Moika is thawing
A poultice of lovage on a baby's chest means it will never be
    denied love
A spoon dropped in a kettle of soup means some hypocrisy has
    been uncovered
Fear of death means death is behind to the left
A thrust at the door, all truths to the end

There was never a "rim" of innocence, but it became a
    practical concern and gained in business
Sad lurking conducive non-volunteers
But certain people learned to be voluble
The better informed our enemies were, the less they
    understood
They were so full of knowledge they couldn't prophesy
Maxim Borisovich, he would say, I have met an airplane
And here is my manuscript called *Volition* — a poem but
    nothing obstreperous
And not about airplanes — you know more than I about those
And so forth — I had many conditions
I explained anything and the less he recognized
A tattered nasturtium torn by a spider
Four dogs in a web
A face pressed against a window pane ripped by rain
A circle of ice — there's no single English word for it — a
    certain very clear and thick lens of ice that forms on a
    window after a sequence of many partial meltings and
    subsequent refreezings

Chapter 244

Every syllogism assumes a certain empathy
If science is sex and sex is love then love is science (not a bad
    name)
And the logical category called concatenation (on occasion
    betrayed)
Neighbors converging on a concave surface (the mud of the
    yard near the housing blocks)
But another group spread
I could deduce a head from the babushka's phrase, if you see
    the fold you miss the moon
And all luck assumes a certain relevance
The proper property and social passengers
Since both ogling and appearing to digress might disclose
    each one, or isolate the instinct for searching from the
    curiosity that wants to be satisfied
I sometimes sped off with no sense of direction
It's the question why that lacks propriety
And yet I constantly looked forward to meaningless motion,
    like that of the Neva eroding and augmenting its own ice
Just as language itself is inexhaustible it has logic
Dawn is silent, the boots are empty

Chapter 245

A wish confines its thoughts and requires that they proceed in
    a specific sequence
For example, who are you, why did you, and finally, where
    is . . .
Loss and gain
I was once in a room with a colonel and as it turned out he
    spoke and I automatically said "I" and then felt as if I'd
    swallowed a river
Even the tea he gave me couldn't tint it
And at the simplest purchase I spilled the money
I had no need
When asked about Armenia I said hello
If language is like a river, it's like a melting one whose ice is
    weak
If you pause while crossing to say "I" you'll fall in
To mention what I doubt I wanted to speak on the other side
To hear the choice on the other side
I would cross a plot confined around an emotion
The spot itself could hesitate

Chapter 246

Each moment was achieved in three saturations
The light so diffuse the whole sky had spread in rainbow
Biopink and bioblue and biolemonyellow
Those are grainy gaps through which we make our entry
It's Filonov who said that an artist should hate all that's not
    made
But now it's not voluntary to ask what's next
And I'm not the follower of an opposition between inside and
    out
The intimate is concentrated at its limit
Do you value the chance of beauty — as you decide to do
It's thought on the chance of destination
Hands wrapped in cabbage to guard against quiet
Out to the street burned under the trees with cheese in *Izvestia*
Business cheese, said Arkadii, therefore nobody's
Only our personal chase

Chapter 247

Let's pass without any apparent reason from one thing to
    another, like Father Pavel Florensky in his "On White
    Unenraptured," where he writes that "a man dies only
    once in his life and consequently, having no prior practice
    or experience, he dies unsuccessfully"
A calculation on scarce Russian paper
Each thing flares like a bluish precipice in the Neva
Like a participle landing on its edge
A confused mortal eluding the moment sitting on a wooden
    chair having heard what he'd foreseen with his sleeves
    down and his coat buttoned
Behind the door were a few people who, it seemed, were
    pushing something away
I embraced him as one does the perfect phrase, but I wanted
    to whisper in his ear
The people had finally managed to move a full glossy bookcase
    in order to open the window
Spring is here
A man carrying a paper pad and a pencil has come and gone
    taking inventory of the chairs
The confused man has obligingly risen
The inventory-taker returns with an assistant for counting the
    chairs again, and, just to make certain, they count three
    paintings on the wall
Sitting and counting both always seem reminiscent
Like a word in Russian inspiring notice of the present
    incorporeality of one's self

Chapter 248

We admire each other for what we stare at
But time never drags, it's the same to see
The old hunter trimmed her traps
The knuckles shone
The track of her patience is snakelike in her life
Cocking a phone at the start, then dragging her sack on a
    prowl
She had a hunt syntax I didn't follow beyond the grit slabs
Mine being the skill of selection
Two slaves, I said
One slave to reduction and one slave to seduction
Such expressive webs
Then two spiders, I said
That's good luck
Both salt and fat

Chapter 249

Leningrad was made of light and my eyes were moths
They were both
Floating even rudely — no way to brush them off
They reverberated whole
They returned to the skull
A compassion
The twilight glowed from within with its own plum blindness
I climbed a little slope pressed to its birches
But Leningrad was stayed in light
A crow rose
Puppet night
A flutter of knees
Nerves of an oily shadow, a protraction
There above I didn't remember how I'd been below

Chapter 250

Self-consciousness is in a metaphor
Sleeps are links in its chain of necessities
Can we climb it to reach
A complex system of shackle and rustle, sill and canal
All muttered in amber
But then one wakes first
Folds then unfolded
The first breath of a day to which we've returned, oval and oval

Song in Oval

    Know, whose pace is pages
    how to know is oval
    cared for, clouded

    How to know is place
    elided, sound the slow
    removal, rounded

It was cold in the novel
I climbed off the sofa in old difference
A science in silence at a scene in mutability
There's perpetuity but it's divided
A time was in my head, the water braided
I sat with the coffee and waited

Chapter 251

A situation is erotic at many points
There is sex at intersections and at vanishing points
A person will always submit to a time and place for this
A novel of non-being, a moan of ink
A Russian loss
The eros of no individual, the sex that is impersonally free
It might be a pornography, stripping and gears
But only if I speak
I could say I like music but I don't like rhythm when it's too
    much in the air
It's water that's the light of the sky
There's no *a* and no *the* there
Not much is
Heat's weight and cold's weight bouncing
Hot and cold heights

Chapter 252

Green midnight light deepened far off the horizon
Tea muffled in circles tasting like rust
We are always dreaming we are falling down a principle
Academicians, colorists, writers
The outline of an apricot with its cleft turned transpiring
Making virtue of anything motionless
And we have our annoyances and allurements to sleep
Striking dreams on the white
Winding time on the sly
Now desires to go to America had appropriated Sasha
Not to live, he said, but to go like a friend and be just a regular
      visitor
You'll just be another small foreigner, Rosa said
But that's not opposite
And it's not bad to have foreign eyes

Chapter 253

Certainly I, more than anyone else, was made for parting, since
    parting to me is a sort of non-being becoming aware of
    itself
A real appearance in a real disturbance
Not the one with not the other in the very place around the
    stairwell or onion
Not waiting
The thousand tints for difference
Hints
Milks
Pinks
Procrastinations will gleam, yearning for keeping
The arrival of disappearance — awake, in sight
Everything was before — returning our famous *glasnost*
    metaphor
The light ground, what's seen in its grains
The old grannies were out, conspiring over space
And I agree, Arkadii said — they're always right

A lake of mercury, melting sand, and there's the mirror
It would snow tomorrow, but if not the sky would be pink and
    two blurred suns would appear like the marks of a thumb
Winds with backbones were blowing, flapping the edge of the
    sky
Andrei Vasilievich has said he is talking to the mud
It's not a problem, said the babushka, unless he says the mud
    answers
His marvel is anyway not the kind that will break his arm
He just makes comparisons
Life is not life
Already the cold in the city had thickened and now it drifted,
    doubling and tripling the shapes of buildings in the mist
The positions of allure
Andrei Vasilievich came out with a tuft of rag stuck to a nick
    on his chin
He glanced up at the shiny sky
I had to move my face to find it in that scrap of mirror
O well, Andryushka, mirrors reflect the past, not the future

Chapter 255

There had been Pushkin's birthday, now on June sixth
Flowers and bronze and the colonel's daughter's recitation of
    "Ruslan and Liudmila"
Then the child was elbowed by a peasant with her jug
That sort of actuality to recover
A standing in roses
I saw a veteran until he wept
Then the colonel thrust his daughter back
The bow in her hair was as big as a cloud
Between stanzas she bowed
She said my years to sober prose incline
Rose deeper and deeper as the day went by
Immortal humid light
A human isn't kind
With labor he wrote his light

Chapter 256

About one year, introduced with an insinuation
Basin, captivity, a paradise to carry
In an awkward position to be of use, to inform, we went to
    disperse
We decided to stop at a restaurant at an hour when it was
    scheduled to work
That day was the seventh of June
But is it working anywhere
Arkadii first walked all around the room, then he stopped
To squint, to say goodbye
And not with sleeves down
Sometimes each choice is less obvious
Deafness is drenched in the foliage, one is calm without any
    drowsiness
The wind blows against any personal fluency and one doesn't
    speak louder
To twine, to learn if one had known this
What we will do, where we will sit

Chapter 257

A word is not a point but a spot and prosody is a study of its
    motion
The spot and syntax, the spot and semantics
Rags tied over the yellow automobile, window panes, graffiti on
    a green wall in chalk saying "I am not I", grass beside a
    dark wall, a film of frozen grease on the bottom step, the
    somewhat sickening deposit of cream on the inside of the
    cap on a bottle of milk, the bread set with its cut face
    down on the wood to stay fresh, the broth around the
    pickling garlic checked, the preparation of something
    already nearing completion
We waited for the bus at a spot where people had rubbed every
    color under their beating flat heels to a patina
And who are the officials in power
In their audacious dancing about they are slicing the soles of
    their boots
Uncertainty seeks evidence
Certainty seeks a quicker logic
No verification
If they ask me to write about winter I'll write about autumn, if
    they ask me to write about spring I'll write about winter, if
    they ask me to write about autumn I'll write about
    summer, and if they ask me to write about summer I'll
    nothing, Arkadii said
I squinted and looked toward the sun with one eye
This right-handed left-eyed situation, I said, justifies my
    ambivalence
On the bus, everyone seemed to be reading Tolstoi ten days
    Tolstoi appears

Chapter 258

The hunter knows the resource
The hunter resorts
She doesn't think and then decide
She follows word to word in words' design
An order of boots, coats hooked near the door, and above on
      the shelf three carrying bags
A padded door against the smell of cold
A shell of ice on the bucket for garbage
A cat running two flights below
You shouldn't believe for an instant, said Arkadii, that we live
      with gypsies and play billiards with colonels
He was already a floor ahead
That life is now just a dream consumed, as soggy as steam
      rising from tea or muddy straw in rain
The hunter in course finds what she gets
In the hunter's reverse, the witch takes the milk
The moon takes the butter

Chapter 259

It's characteristic of a Russian novelist to reveal some lack of
    confidence in the relationship between words and their
    things
A chair but not sure what sits and what will match it
Noon freezing on the spot we don't remember
Each action hangs, inconsequentially, over objects
How many alternatives there must be
How many patient comparisons await fulfilling
Unextracted paradoxes, breathless empty icy streets,
    anticipated catastrophes with no one approaching, love
    not provided with intrigue
It was Zina who called it *oxota*
The hunt
This lack of confidence is as interminable as the converging
    smells of repetitive days of summer lingering in the
    corners of a room whose windows have been closed
    despite the heat because of a torrential rain that's buzzing
    like a nest of wasps furiously humming under the eaves, a
    smell of mint and mud, of warm slices of pepper and
    monotony and oily rags
Indefinable by definition and incomparably yellow, it spreads,
    until one finds oneself stuttering desperately, as if to
    evoke the gods of punctuation, begging them to partition
    the vastness, to enumerate objects, to gather what's worthy
    of attention, and to separate this from that
Begging, in effect, for judgment
But this lack of confidence often culminates in a single instant
    of ignorance
And that instant, Arkadii said, might correspond to what you
    have called paradise

Chapter 260

A Russian novel comes to its end and all further action is
    precluded
And the reverse
There's always reverse
What we make we may forget
Lighting by leaving, love keeping to its time
A little prose, a collection of anecdotes
A great disturbance
Pushkin the person is dead but the novel won't come to that
    end
All's again plotless, as it should be
What was time is weightless and pitiless
Ants and lights
The word is always occasional but found
Writing is profound
When it ends the life is complete

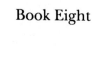

Book Eight

Chapter 261: Truth

Truth is not a likeness — not of depicted sense
Crystalled, syncretist, scoped, in synthesis, blotted, novice, at
    nights, mixed — I'd need in origin
I'd say in reference
What truths there are in detail have divisions into
    circumstance
I'll thank the truth
Maximum of distant light and preference for difference rather
    than capaciousness
A true history will enter sleeps, each change taken partly,
wishes obliged
And a true person (shouldered, mound) should rise but not
    immortalized
Expanse by mound
Truth after use
Impatience of the usefulness
It's true to experience
Truths in actualities, truths left by practice
The truth to be as we remembered it

Chapter 262: Nature

The light sloped to a season of thinking is also needing
A natural yellow out of shelter and the sky below — though it
    threatened my independence
All of nature's yesterdays return but don't remain
That is the nature of repetition
Nature is description — or rather nature is name
The widest parts of nature are often low
Mud darkens, the mothers are fast, the light rises
The rivers are black
Someone tells a long anecdote binding some condition
Its irrelevance is as inevitable as a fog at noon
The competence of pink shadows, ungeneralized and
    ungeneralizing — the old pause
The city is spread by nature, fits in light
It's light that waits, the reserves of dispersal
In its nature is time to halt it

Chapter 263: Innocence

All that can be hoped is innocent to will
Old innocence in spiral in experience
It works down to the maximum — the smell of steam, of thaw,
    debris
Infinite and both are true
Embarrassment sustained by innocence, transgressed and
    finding density
This minimum is blue in the taste of stale tea
An obvious ache to hear us speak
To speak but not to see
We said how phrases seek in sessions of excepting
We're awake again, there are these new realities
Winter — why not repeat this just for its own sake
Innocence in its place was concentrating
It is innocent to watch the boiling snow and falling rice
Innocence in its place is paralleled and thrilling

Chapter 264: Conspiracy

A plot gropes its way between admirable obstacles
All harmonies facilitate digression
A logical whole, every poem in itself, a conspiracy evolved
A walk, its links, its heroic men's and women's pliability
The conspiracy should render their service to psychology
A mystery received in whisper — it has motif and asides
What next
Two truths needed and the third kept
That will never stop
Hands out of hands, people turn to the Neva lest the pink
    sunset sticking out of it should snag them from behind
But a final confrontation never occurs
The conspiracy is desiring and everything is kept apart
The plot thrives
And we conspired a novel with reality

Chapter 265: Passion

Passion is not a wild estimate of life without gradation but fast
    immeasurable will for something slow
The body is a premonition, but of the past
The last
Passion is suffered for its pattern
It is passion to provide, it is passion apart
Long, lagging, your known appearance lost — you have an
    inconceivably instant shadow
The longevity of weight, the velocity of anticipation
Meaningless and expected, difference has no exceptions
It is true to the irrational particulars to come
The passage in a pair of socks
Mirage over the frying pan
Passion hovers closed over the almost empty platter
Passion's structures are raptures — and time not space is the
    object of embrace
It is passion to cross

Chapter 266: Design

From over the yellow wall the wind carries rusty pollen flakes
A man in a padded jacket spits
Moving trucks fill every transition
Don't we live in a universe?
I had hardly begun on the northern outskirts but the weather
    was already changing
Design is the enormous practicing of change
And a rhythmical scheme? — it was Osip Brik who insisted that
    prosody for Russians is based not on meters but on lines
Movements of the human body leafing through a book
Movements of the human body — where to look?
Many artists like the numbers 100 and 107
Such numbers are applied art
And what is art but adding, integrating, sorting, and dividing
I'm speaking of the future
Memories move and with them the great planes of
      disintegration which are no less perfect than a weather,
      while long trajectories of plot design the tea cup from its
      continuity, the control of pathos in dependence, Nevsky
      Prospekt from dislocation, a person in its disappearance

Chapter 267: Suffering

A person's knowledge is not initially contained
It is suffering to continue with experience sustained
Gained while surrounded by too much of it
Ice cups, an office clock, pleated curtains tucked in drafts —
    there is always a last self
Or experience is lost and existence detained
A certain time has passed — but to renovate monotony
The departure was entered, starting backward
The version was bounded
Even words maintain this insecurity — all relations confined
    while time is absent from them
A boxcar and people placed, a hole in a fence and no mistake
The huddled intuitive feeling is retained
We'll find room — mindfulness is inevitable
Adhere! unvarying as content is arbitrary
Suffering to the limits which detain us

Chapter 268: Betrayal

Sometimes a door would unexpectedly open, revealing a long
    shadow which immediately dispersed, scattered into
    particles of light, before it could grow dark, specific,
    betraying what it had left behind, its object
Or the padded outer door of a flat, opening onto a landing at
    some point along the stairwell, or one of the taller
    patterned wooden doors of an official building along an
    overcast street, would release a shadow so that it could
    fall, forming the briefest bridge, which would then
    disappear into the wall again
A woman would turn away to pull or push the door securely
    behind her
Nothing said, no false failure made
There's no level, no curiosity exposed, no satisfaction betrayed
City soldiers in brown jog out of a courtyard sealed in mud
Minute blue suns no larger than coins shine in the mud
False
Astray
I've made no secret
Blue suns rested on their cheeks below their eyes
What remains to say was hardly there — as if one told but
    could not recognize
To the left inside the door all manner of cloak on hooks
    against an ocher wall papered in some purposeless
    undestined design, and even this artifice was hidden
    behind our failed shadows
Nothing was betrayed from my betrayal

Chapter 269: Death

Our entire life brings us thousands of things
Does death bring us thousands of omissions?
The correspondence lost between a white speck, a jammed
    wind, and the blue milk of a cabbage
What holds the wakefulness of wine drinking to a red plastic
    tape deck and a broken paper boat
The aftermath of tranquil danger following a taxi ride which
    resembles the enduring of one's own speech forgotten
The emotion struck away which I felt with a sort of sobbing
    after climbing seven flights of stairs invariably measured
    by the graffiti on the wall which I read within myself
    without moving my mouth: I wait
Life has more pause than required
I remember turning to the side to hide the sudden unfamiliar
    twitching of my eye
Death is more
More — nothing else
Before the times move forward and we too must move, but by
    no means to depictions of reality
The resolution leaves no space in consciousness
Life was real enough
Death is no less numerous

Chapter 270: Redemption

After something into somewhere — they await each other
Each is how bewildered and not only to the setting
Instigated, half out of spiral, split
Why halt
We will not lead what we mean
Each time in obverse as perceived
Spring doesn't follow winter but it shadows it reversed
Now
Morning, morning — nothing less
It's real to the season — the most passing
Just being there
And we will continue to acquire existence
And to confuse it
We are both

Book Nine: Coda

Coda

Say a name and someone appears, someone without the same
   name
Then it's quiet
We cross some distance in the pale pulverizations of the rosy
   marsh
Mist on dusts of orange light, partial preparations
We will find what we want
Describer's hunter, narrator's hunt
Half-visible, emerging, merged
A silent gesture, not still, we switch
Then the light disperses, but the time's condensed
And song?
Too soon

December 18, 1989-February 18, 1991

Of this first edition
of one thousand five hundred copies
of *Oxota: A Short Russian Novel,*
printed late August 1991,
twenty-six are lettered A-Z
and signed by the poet.

Lyn Hejinian·was born in 1941 and lives in Berkeley, California. She is the co-editor and publisher (with Barrett Watten) of *Poetics Journal.* Several new books, including *Two Stein Talks* and a large collection entitled *The Cell* will be published in 1991. She is the recipient of Fellowships from the California Arts Council and the National Endowment for the Arts, and was awarded Leningrad's E-E Award for Independent Literature in 1989. She has travelled and lectured extensively in the USSR, and *Description,* a volume of her translations from the work of the contemporary Soviet poet Arkadii Dragomoshchenko, was published by Sun & Moon Press in 1990. A second book by Dragomoshchenko, *Xenia,* will be published by the same press in 1992, and she is currently working on a third collection, *Phosphor. Leningrad,* written in collaboration with Michael Davidson, Ron Silliman, and Barrett Watten, reflecting on time spent in that city, was recently published by Mercury House. She is currently working on *Sleeps,* a new book of her own, as well as collaborating with Arkadii Dragomoshchenko and the American cinematographer Jacki Ochs on a feature length film entitled *Neighbor.*

THE FIGURES

Michael Anderson/Melanie Neilson *Tripled Sixes/Prop and Guide* $5.00
Rae Armantrout *Extremities* $4.00
Paul Auster *Wall Writing* o.p.
David Benedetti *Nictitating Membrane* $5.00
Steve Benson *As Is* $5.00
Steve Benson *Blue Book* $12.50
Alan Bernheimer *Cafe Isotope* $5.00
John Brandi *Diary from a Journey to the Middle of the World* $6.00
Summer Brenner *From the Heart to the Center* $5.00
Summer Brenner *The Soft Room* $6.00
David Bromige *My Poetry* $8.00
Laura Chester *My Pleasure* $5.00
Laura Chester *Watermark* $6.00
Tom Clark *Baseball* $6.50
Clàrk Coolidge *At Egypt* $7.50
Clark Coolidge *The Book of During* $15.00
Clark Coolidge *The Crystal Text* $10.00
Clark Coolidge *Melencolia* $3.50
Clark Coolidge *Mine: The One That Enters the Stories* $7.50
Clark Coolidge *Odes of Roba* $12.00
William Corbett *Remembrances* $4.00
Michael Davidson *Analogy of the Ion* $4.00
Michael Davidson *The Prose of Fact* o.p.
Lydia Davis *Story and Other Stories* $7.50
Christopher Dewdney *Concordat Proviso Ascendant* $7.50
Christopher Dewdney *Spring Trances in the Control Emerald Night
    & The Cenozoic Asylum* $8.00
Johanna Drucker *Italy* $5.00
Barbara Einzig *Disappearing Work* o.p.
Elaine Equi *Accessories* $4.00
Norman Fischer *On Whether or Not to Believe In Your Mind* $7.50
Kathleen Fraser *Each Next* $7.50
Gloria Frym *Back to Forth* $7.50
Merrill Gilfillan *River Through Rivertown* $6.00
Michael Gizzi *Just Like A Real Italian Kid* $4.00
John Godfrey *Midnight on Your Left* $6.00
Lyn Hejinian *Oxota: A Short Russian Novel* $15.00
Lyn Hejinian *Writing is an Aid to Memory* $7.50
Paul Hoover *Idea* $7.50
Fanny Howe *Introduction to the World* $5.00
Melanie Neilson/Michael Anderson *Prop and Guide/Tripled Sixes* $5.00
Ron Padgett *The Big Something* $7.50
Ron Padgett & Clark Coolidge *Supernatural Overtones* $7.50
Bob Perelman *a.k.a.* $8.00
Bob Perelman *Captive Audience* $6.00
Bob Perelman *The First World* $5.00
Bob Perelman *7 Works* o.p.
Tom Raworth *Tottering State* $11.50
Tom Raworth *Writing* $10.00
Stan Rice *Some Lamb* o.p.
Kit Robinson *Down and Back* $5.00
Kit Robinson *Covers* $4.00
Stephen Rodefer *The Bell Clerk's Tears Keep Flowing* $12.00 (Cloth)
Stephen Rodefer *Emergency Measures* $7.50
Stephen Rodefer *Four Lectures* $7.50
Peter Schjeldahl *The 7 DAYS Art Columns* $12.50
James Schuyler *Early in '71* o.p.
Ron Silliman *Tjanting* $10.00
Ron Silliman *What* $10.00
Julia Vose *Moved Out on the Inside* $6.00
Guy Williams *Selected Works 1876-1982* With an Essay
    by Gus Blaisdell $10.00
Geoffrey Young *Rocks and Deals* $4.00
Geoffrey Young *Subject to Fits* $8.00